THE ENLIGHTENED WILL SHINE

SUNY Series in Judaica: Hermeneutics, Mysticism, and Religion
Michael Fishbane, Robert Goldenberg, and Elliot Wolfson, editors

THE ENLIGHTENED WILL SHINE

Symbolization and Theurgy in the Later Strata of the Zohar

by
Pinchas Giller

State University of New York Press

Published by
State University of New York Press, Albany

Printed in the United States of America

For information, address the State University of New York Press,
State University Plaza, Albany, NY 12246

Production by Christine Lynch
Marketing by Theresa A. Swierzowski

Library of Congress Cataloging-in-Publication Data

Giller, Pinchas, 1953–
The enlightened will shine : symbolization and theurgy in the later strata of the Zohar / by Pinchas Giller
p. cm. — (SUNY series in Judaica)
Includes bibliographical references and index.
ISBN 0-7914-1711-5.— ISBN 0-7914-1712-3 (pbk.)
1. Tikkunei Zohar. 2. Ra'aya mehemana. 3. Cabala—History.
I. Title. II. Series.
BM525.A6T5738 1993
296.1'6—dc20 92-44705
CIP

10 9 8 7 6 5 4 3 2 1

For My Parents

Contents

Acknowledgments

This work was originally presented as a doctoral thesis for the Graduate Theological Union in Berkeley, California. Many thanks to Daniel C. Matt, my advisor, for his patience and wisdom in the face of many frenzied telephone calls. Thanks, as well, to my thesis committee: Robert Alter, David Biale, and Hilary Martin.

This work would not have been completed without the efforts of Ronni Hendel, Joshua Kosman, Jennifer Sylvor, and Jonathan Zemke, who tirelessly and unselfishly read and re-read early and late drafts, midwifing its transition into English. Norma Schneider was generous with her time in advising how the thesis should be made into a book. I must thank Elliot Wolfson, who similarly read and commented exhaustively on this text during all stages of its preparation. Ira Robinson, of Concordia University, has been most supportive of my efforts to complete this work on time. Also, thank you, Ronni, for being so patient.

Transliterations

a,e	alef	l	lamed
b	bet	m	mem
v	vet	n	nun
g	gimmel	s	samekh
d	dalet	’	ayin
h	he	p	pe
v	vav	f	fe
z	zayin	ẓ	zadi
ḥ	het	q,k	qof
t	tet	r	resh
y,i	yod	sh	shin
k	kaf	s	sin
kh	khaf	t	tav

Abbreviations

MhZ	Isaiah Tishby and Fishel Lachover. *Mishnat ha-Zohar* [The Teaching of the Zohar], 2 vols. Jerusalem: Mossad Bialik, 1971.
RM	*Ra'aya Meheimna*, in *Sefer ha-Zohar*, Reuven Margaliot, etc.
TZ	*Tiqqunei ha-Zonar*, Reuven Margaliot (Jerusalem: Mossad Ha-Rav Kook, 1978); also *Tiqqunei ha-Zohar* (Orta Koj: 1740), *Tiqqunei ha-Zohar* (Bzhitomir: 1873).
TZḤ	*Tiqqunim*, in *Zohar Ḥadash*, ed. Reuven Margaliot. Jerusalem: Mossad Ha-Rav Kook, 1978.
(TZ)	Material by the author of *Tiqqunei ha-Zohar* and *Ra'aya Meheimna*, which is placed anonymously in other parts of the Zohar.
Z I, II, III	*Sefer ha-Zohar*, ed. Reuven Margaliot, 3 vols., 4th ed. Jerusalem: Mossad Ha-Rav Kook, 1964.

Preface

This study—of a pair of voluminous works of medieval Jewish mysticism—consists of an analysis of the use of symbolism and theurgy in the texts *Tiqqunei ha-Zohar* (or the *Tiqqunim*) and *Ra'aya Meheimna*. Although these texts have been viewed by scholars as secondary to the rest of the Zohar, they have been particularly beloved by kabbalists themselves. This study demonstrates the significance of their doctrinal contributions to theosophical Kabbalah.

I was initially attracted to these works because of a discrepancy between their traditional currency and the scholarly attitude toward them. There was a tendency, among critical scholars, to dismiss them as derivative or otherwise secondary to the "main" sections of the Zohar. At the same time, they were apparently well beloved by many generations of kabbalists, with more editions of *Tiqqunei ha-Zohar* being produced than of the Zohar itself. I set out, initially, to investigate the attraction of these texts for the traditional community. The first chapter of this study distinguishes between the main sections of the Zohar and the material considered *Tiqqunei ha-Zohar* and *Ra'aya Meheimna*.

The second chapter addresses the author's use of kabbalistic symbolism. The anonymous author of these works presents a unified world-view that is unique and highly influential in the subsequent development of Jewish mysticism. The hermeneutical methodology of *Tiqqunei ha-Zohar* is based on this author's conception of the *kinnui*, or symbolic euphemism, as the basis of his associative method. The *kinnui* is the device through which traditional Jewish motifs are transformed into metaphysical symbols. This process of symbolization underlies the relationship of the mystic and religious authority. The author's tendency to "read" his doctrinal additions into preexistent Zoharic texts was important in the development of kabbalistic hermeneutics. This practice prefigured the methodology of much later exegesis of the Zohar.

The third chapter of this study examines the notion of a vocation of Jewish mystics, the *maskilim*. In the *Tiqqunim*, the *maskil*, or enlightened mystic, is the agent and interpreter of religious truth. The order of the *maskilim* recognizes the Zohar as its mystical charter. Mystical illumination and enlightenment came from the practice of contemplative Torah study, utilizing the symbolic hermeneutic of the theosophical Kabbalah.

Tiqqunei ha-Zohar and *Ra'aya Meheimna* portray the world as caught in an unfolding drama of catastrophe and mythic chaos. The author uses certain midrashic and Zoharic traditions in a judicious and characteristic manner that distinguishes them from the rest of the Zohar. The fourth chapter of this study will present the author's myth of prehistory, which is based largely on the sagas of the fall of Adam and the flood. The flood accounts are metaphors for the present experience of humankind, which is distinguished by qualities of brokenness and disorder. The heightened social and soteric roles of the enlightened mystic, as well as the author's use of images of struggle, brokenness, and distension, have great effect on the development of subsequent kabbalistic movements and doctrines.

Contemporary scholars have compared the role of the mystic to that of the legalist, to the detriment of the latter. This has led to some misinterpretation of the author's relationship to the legal tradition, which the fifth chapter of this study attempts to resolve. In fact, the author makes judicious use of the tropes of Jewish law, so that the mystic's vocation at times overlaps with that of the legalist. In the light of this extensive use of legal material, this study demonstrates that the author harbored no antinomian attitude toward the law. This study further demonstrates that, far from being ambivalent, *Tiqqunei ha-Zohar* and *Ra'aya Meheimna* portray a unified view of this mystic's inner world.

The sixth and seventh chapters analyze the theurgic character of the *Tiqqunim* and *Ra'aya Meheimna*. These works responded to the dilemmas posed by the myth of chaos with a theurgic religious practice that made wide use of his erudition in *halakhah*, Jewish law. The author's reinterpretations of halakhic dicta and rhetoric reflected the conditions of the fall and the flood. His use of rabbinical law and lore contradicts the scholarly opinion that there is an antinomian strain in his thought. An investigation of the rabbinic dimension of the *Tiqqunim* is particularly important, as the work's ascent to liturgical and canonical status is due to the perceived authenticity of the author's interpretation of classical Judaism.

The specific contribution of this work lies in a number of areas. The author's symbolization of halakhic material is unique and has not yet been dealt with in a conclusive manner. In fact, although the deep traditionalism of the theosophical kabbalah has been demonstrated by Gershom Scholem and his students, there have been, to date, few analyses of the relationship of specific areas of *halakhah* and the Zohar. The clarification of the author's ambilavent attitude to rabbinic authority is long overdue. The identification of a model of mystical behavior, which is such a constant theme in the *Tiqqunim*, is also a new area of research. Ideally, this study will serve as a modest bridging of the gap between critical scholars of this tradition and its pietistic practitioners, through understanding the author's accomodation of rabbinic religious tradition into his mystical world-view.

1

Tiqqunei ha-Zohar and *Ra'aya Meheimna* in Context

The enlightened will shine like the brightness of the firmament (Daniel 12:3). *The enlightened* are Rabbi Shimon and his companions, *will shine* when they gathered together, they were permitted an audience with Elijah, all the souls of the academy and all the hidden and cerebral angels. And the Most Transcendent permitted all the holy names and beings and all the signs to reveal their hidden secrets to them, every name on its own level, and the ten *sefirot* were permitted to reveal to them secrets hidden until the advent of the Messiah.

—*Tiqqunei ha-Zohar* 1a

The main sections of the Zohar were composed informally, based on (the sages') discussion when they had completed studying the intricacies of the laws of the Torah. But for *Tiqqunei ha-Zohar* and *Ra'aya Meheimna,* the Song of Songs, *Piqqudim* and the *Idra,* they truly put everything aside for the present text, for these compositions complete the others. In it, they delved into the secrets that came forth to them, of the *shining of the firmament . . .*

—Moshe Cordovero[1]

The purpose of this study is to examine two works of an anonymous medieval Jewish mystic: *Tiqqunei ha-Zohar* (also called the *Tiqqunim)* and *Ra'aya Meheimna.* Both works are included in the *Zohar,* the classical work of Jewish mysticism. The author of the *Tiqqunim* was one of the last of the circle of scholars who composed the Zohar. This mystic's expressive style and theological ideas stand out from the rest of the Zohar. His works have a particular understanding of the mystic's role in society. The author of the *Tiqqunim* and *Ra'aya Meheimna* was very conscious of the tensions inherent in the mystic's relationship to Jewish law and society. When considered together, the works of this mystic have a coherent and unified theological position that encompasses the dominant themes of Jewish mysticism up to his time and presage its subsequent historical development. This study will examine this obscure figure and show his effect on subsequent Jewish spirituality.

The Zohar literature is the strongest expression of the medieval Jewish mysticism that is commonly called *Kabbalah.* The Hebrew word *kabbalah* means, literally, "that which is received." This emphasis on reception reflects a tension between adherence to traditional religious structures and lore, on the one hand, and the renewal of the tradition through creative reinterpretation, on the other.[2] Kabbalists reviewed the vast exoteric Jewish tradition and understood its inner dynamics in novel and compelling ways. The legal (*halakhic*) and homiletic (*aggadic*) structure of Rabbinic Judaism provided Kabbalah with its imagery, whereas its religious practices defined the parameters of the kabbalist's experience. The strength of the Kabbalah lay in its perceived authenticity, in its evocation of the spirit of the law. Its theorists generally adhered to the most pious belief and practice. Kabbalistic truths, therefore, are best understood in the context of their source tradition, for Kabbalah is the product of a reconsideration of the universe of symbols provided by classical Judaism.

Although reinforcing the values and piety of Rabbinic Judaism, Kabbalah expressed the mystical desire for renewed experience of the transcendent and for the metaphysical understanding of reality. Kabbalists claimed to experience the metaphysical ultimacies as well as the historical realities of Judaism. Kabbalah portrayed itself as the inner component of Judaism, the resolution of its underlying paradoxes and contradictions.

The Zohar is the preeminent text of the theosophical Kabbalah, the first great work of genius in this tradition. The Zohar is not a single work, but a collection of some two dozen separate compositions, constituting, in published editions, over 2,000 pages of closely printed Aramaic text. These various compositions experiment with a number of writing styles and rabbinic literary forms. Such stylistic variety may be either the result of multiple authors and strata of composition or the attempt of a single author to find his literary muse.[3] Because of the sophistication of their ideas and their late setting, *Tiqqunei ha-Zohar* and *Ra'aya Meheimna* probably make up the latest chronological stratum of the Zohar.

Critical Zohar studies, to date, have concentrated on the main body of the Zohar, which is generally understood as having been compiled by R. Moshe Ben Shem Tov de Leon, of late thirteenth century Guadalajara, Spain. Contemporary scholars of Kabbalah, such as Gershom Scholem, Isaiah Tishby, and Yehudah Liebes have posited a process of literary development that can be charted within the confusion of the Zohar's structure. According to this "documentary hypothesis," the mysticism of the Zohar developed from a system based in philosophy to one based in theosophy. *Midrash ha-Ne'elam,* which Scholem and Tishby considered the earliest material, presents the idea of communities of mystic rabbis. In later compositions, the mise-en-scène became more detailed, while the theosophical nature became more pronounced, so that the strongest literary compositions were those in which the mystical ideas were most clearly and daringly formulated. The culminating texts of the Zohar are the *Idrot,* which describe convocations in which several of the participants reveal anthropomorphic visions of the Godhead and perish in mystical ecstasy.[4]

The literary style and language of the Zohar are unique. Its structure, like other late midrashim such as *Pirqei de-Rabi Eliezer* and *Tanna de-Bei Eliyahu,* shows the unifying vision of a single hand.[5] Often, a section will commence with a homiletic proem based on the static imagery of the Bible's Wisdom literature. In a juxtaposition common to midrashic and medieval homiletical literature, a Pentateuchal exegesis will then be linked to this homily. This proem form was a movement away from the simple exegesis of a proof text toward the discussion of the interaction of the religious symbols in their own right. Although the Zohar's central pretense is that it is a Tannaitic midrash, its rambling, lengthy form and idiosyncratic Aramaic are unlike any other rabbinic creation.

Tiqqunei ha-Zohar (possibly "Infrastructures[6] of the Zohar") is structured around seventy lengthy exegeses of the first sentence of the Bible.[7] Additional sections of *Tiqqunim* were collected and published in the *Zohar Ḥadash*, an anthology of texts that were not included in initial editions of the Zohar.[8] The main text of *Tiqqunei ha-Zohar* is more powerful and coherent than the material in the *Zohar Ḥadash*, which might have been considered secondary by the earliest editors, if not by the author himself.[9] *Tiqqunei ha-Zohar* was first published in Mantua in 1658.The Orta Koj edition (1719) represents editorial decisions originating in the school of the great theorist of Lurianic Kabbalah, Hayyim Vital, by way of his student Hayyim Alfandari. This edition has served as the basis for most use of the *Tiqqunim* in subsequent Jewish intellectual history. Its dominance is even more complete than that of the Mantua-Vilna edition of the Zohar. Even so, it is clear that the Orta Koj edition is full of additions by later editors.

The *Tiqqunim* themselves are monographs that flow into one another. Each *Tiqqun* is a homily that begins with the Hebrew *Bereshit*, or "In the Beginning." A given *Tiqqun* may veer off in a number of directions or exhaustively explore one subject.[10] The *Tiqqunim* abandon the format of the "mystical novel,"[11] employed by the most literarily successful sections of the Zohar, in favor of an unstructured associative method. The author sometimes seems to delight in his opaque style, in which the logical connections between subjects are often unclear. His cascade of images often resembles a process of free association. The *Tiqqunim* present a fevered melange, whose symbolic elements are drawn from mythic *aggadot,* philosophical terms, Divine names, linguistic mysticism, and rabbinic legal dicta. As scraps and fragments of these various traditions are invoked and discarded, the reader is obliged to reconstruct the nuances of the associative flow. This associative method underscores the author's spiritual obsessions, as he returns repeatedly to the themes that preoccupy him.

The second treatise by the author of *Tiqqunei ha-Zohar* is called *Ra'aya Meheimna,* or "The Faithful Shepherd." The *Ra'aya Meheimna* is composed in the form of a "book of commandments" (*sefer miẓvot*), a popular genre of medieval Jewish writing. Books of commandments were produced by such seminal figures as Maimonides, Naḥmanides, and Menaḥem Recanati. They commonly listed the commandments in the Torah and divulged their inner nature. In accordance with the conventions of this genre, every section of the *Ra'aya Meheimna* is centered around a particular commandment.[12] The "faithful shepherd," Moses, is exhorted by the members of the celestial academy to explain the mystical nature of the commandments, particularly, in the extant sections, the commandments regarding the sacrificial cult. This text has a more coherent literary structure than the rambling, associative *Tiqqunim.*[13]

The dialogues recorded in *Ra'aya Meheimna* and the *Tiqqunim* take place after the deaths of Shimon bar Yoḥai and his companions, in the heavenly academy. Participants include, among others, the prophet Elijah, Moses, the incarnate *Shekhinah,* and God. There are references to the specific lore of the Zohar: to persons such as the legendary Rabbi Cruspedai,[14] to the events of the *Idrot,*[15] and to the revelation of the *Zohar.*[16] The author clearly intended to continue the romantic tradition of the Zohar and subsequent works such as Joseph of Hamadan's *Sefer Tashaq.*

The author of the *Tiqqunim,* unlike the author of the Zohar, makes little effort to portray himself as anything but a medieval figure.[17] His attempts at pseudepigraphy are half-hearted, so that the *Tiqqunim* and *Ra'aya Meheimna* are riddled with anachronisms. The author often refers to texts that were plainly composed after the era of Shimon Bar Yoḥai. He makes anachronistic references to the *targumim* of Onkelos[18] and Jonathan Ben Uzziel.[19] His references to "Ben Sira"[20] seem to refer to the medieval *Alpha-Beta de-Ben Sira.* A characteristic anachronism, impossible in the Tannaitic period, is the expression *esh nogah,* "glowing light," literally the Spanish *sinagoga,* synagogue.[21] The text also makes references to the Zohar[22] and to itself.[23]

The *Tiqqunim* are, by their own definition, secondary and accessory to the Zohar. Nonetheless, they are important as a bridge between the internal development of the Zohar and the interpretive systems of subsequent kabbalists. As an early reader of the Zohar and as a theorist in the same tradition, their author embodied the values of reception and development inherent in the Kabbalah. Motifs and ideas that are secondary or unstressed in the *Tiqqunim,* thus gaining prominence in the subsequent development of Kabbalah. It has long been customary to deprecate the *Tiqqunim* as inferior, both literarily and theologically, to the rest of the Zohar. It is the aim of this study to show that the *Tiqqunim* played an important part in the acceptance of the Zohar as canonical literature.

2

The Hermeneutics of Theosophical Kabbalah: The Symbolization of Sacred Text

Tiqqunei ha-Zohar is one of the last great works of theosophical Kabbalah.[1] Although there are claims for Tannaitic, Manichean, or Neoplatonic origins for many of the ideas of theosophical Kabbalah, its main locus seems to have been thirteenth- and fourteenth-century Christian Spain. The first theosophical work was the *Sefer ha-Bahir,* a quasi-midrashic text of mysterious origin that first appeared in twelfth-century Provence.[2] These theosophical kabbalists[3] identified an esoteric dimension, an underlying "soul," of Rabbinic Judaism. They also expressed impatience and dissatisfaction with understandings of that Judaism that were overly exoteric and rationalistic.

Theosophical Kabbalah is a mysticism of language; the mystical experience that it authorizes consists of the contemplation of the symbolic repertoire of the Jewish canon. This body of symbols included images and motifs from the Bible and Talmud's universe of narrative, geographical, cultic, and legal material. The symbols are employed to describe God's hypostatic emanation through the *sefirot,* the dimensions or realms of existence.[4]

Religious experience and mystical practice developed from the mystic's encounter with the canonical text, which itself encompassed all existence and metaphysical reality. Theosophical kabbalists saw the Torah as a primordial text, predating the creation of the world,[5] a living garment numinous with potential meaning. Both the *sefirot* and the Divine letters were instruments employed by the kabbalist. The consonantal rendering of the Torah enabled the text to be read with variants or multiple meanings. The essence of the text, however, remained amorphous, in a state of ongoing potentiality, defying limitation.

The rabbinic sanction of multiple understandings of scripture presumed that the Torah was a work of amorphous numinosity. This understanding of the Divine text allowed the kabbalists to continue the creative methodologies of classical midrash. In the same way, the most conservative of rabbinic values considered Torah study and dissemination the central format for enlightenment. Theosophical Kabbalah understood interaction with the Divine text through Torah study as equivalent, in erotic metaphor, with the adherent's union with the ineffable Divine.[6]

The energies of the Divine did not flow into the corporeal world in a set or orderly fashion; the *sefirot* did not interact in a fixed or static way. In fact, relationships between the *sefirot* shifted according to the rhythms of time and the relative ascendancy of the powers of good and evil. The kabbalists tried to understand the patterns of these interactions, as well as the essential nature of the *sefirot*. Biblical verses were understood in terms of the juxtaposition of several symbols, themselves symbolic of various *sefirot*. Subject-predicate relationships and narrative images of movement in the proof text were understood as representing different patterns of sefirotic emanation. This sefirotic conceptualization often canceled the literal meaning of the text, replacing it with descriptions of the mythic function of God's emanation.

The symbolic reading of scripture was intended to convey messages that are not easily communicable in their essence.[7] This function of the symbol was acceptable to even the most conservative theologians when seen in terms of traditional Jewish values of God's ineffability and the final inadequacy of the reader's perception of the Divine. Scriptural texts contained at least two levels of meaning: *nigleh* (the revealed) and *nistar* (the hidden). The Zohar often expressed the tension between these two levels in its image of the *egoz*, or nut, whose inner nature is concealed by an opaque shell.[8] The divine text is both hidden and intellectually accessible. Its network of symbols was both a window to esoteric meaning and an indication of God's ineffable nature. For the mystical adept, contemplation of the symbolic motifs presented by the text was the central means of mystical illumination.

Texts that describe static relationships, such as the dimensions of the Tabernacle, the social roles of the Wisdom literature[9] or biblical genealogies, particularly lent themselves to symbolic interpretation. These overtly dry, irrelevant passages were thought of as encoded with esoteric meaning. The erotic images of the Song of Songs also lent themselves to interpretation in terms of mystical experience. That text's images of erotic longing and pathos had long been allegorized in terms of the Jewish national experience. In the Kabbalah, its eroticism represented the frustrating transience of the quest for mystical union.[10]

Much of this literature was presented in the conventional literary formats of the Middle Ages: scriptural commentaries, books of commandments, and didactic works such as Joseph Gikatilla's *Sha'arei Orah.* Joseph of Hamadan, R. David ben Yehudah ha-Ḥasid, the Zohar, and the works of the author of the *Tiqqunim* represent experiments in the "mystical novel,"anthologies of theosophical interpretations rendered in midrashic form. *Tiqqunei ha-Zohar* and *Ra'aya Mehimna* used the style of dialogue and narrative's developed by the Zohar. They also displayed the didacticism of Gikatilla's works and other guides to symbolic reading of sacred texts.

The Palette of Symbols

Unlike the main sections of the Zohar, which employ narrative and quasi-legalistic literary style, the *Tiqqunim* and, to a lesser extent, *Ra'aya Meheimna* are written in an impressionistic style that approaches stream of consciousness. Religious meaning is determined from the way a symbol is linked to other images and motifs to which it has some formal relation. The chain of association reflects the mental processes of the mystical author. His latent attitudes regarding rabbinic tradition can also be determined from the way that he utilizes aggadic motifs or halakhic dicta.

Tiqqunei ha-Zohar's symbolic repertoire draws on two hermeneutical traditions in particular: the Torah's composition from the various esoteric names of God and the esoteric underpinings of the Masoretic traditions of vocalization and cantillation.[11]

Theosophical Kabbalah struggled with the dilemma of how to express the ineffable. The Jewish philosophical understanding of the nature of God created the need for a conceptual symbol of ineffability, if only to express the limitations of language. The names of God were understood as defining the contours of God's ineffability.

There are various rabbinic traditions of a numinous and dynamic name of God. These traditions are alluded to in such remarks as "The bottomless abyss of all creation is sealed in the name."[12] The ancient traditions of the sacred names of God were handed down by Jewish mystical adepts under conditions of great secrecy.[13] Naḥmanides' statement that "the whole Torah is names of the Blessed Holy One,"[14] awaiting recombination by the mystic adept, represents the emergence of an idea that had been available only to a restricted spiritual elite. Divine names were common to the twelfth-century *ḥasidei ashkenaz*, particularly Eleazer of Worms in his *Sefer ha-Ḥokhmah* and *Sefer ha-Shem.*[15] This tradition of names culminated in the notions of the forty-two- and seventy-two-letter names of God. These esoteric rabbinic traditions had filtered through Geonic circles to the Ḥasidei Ashkenaz, and from there to the Castilean theosophists.[16]

Tiqqunei ha-Zohar and *Ra'aya Meheimna* state that God may be called by all names, but He has no specific name.[17] Holy names are descriptions of action, relating to the creator and his relationship to creation,[18] for "the Master of the World extends through those names and rules through them."[19] One aspect of messianic redemption will be the cessation of *temurot,* the textual distinctions between names and their pronunciations.[20] Idolatry is seen as deriving from the demonization of the holy name YHVH.[21] The author seems to have adopted the kabbalistic traditions of the Divine name, but the ubiquity of the Divine name is ultimately less profound than the general presence of other kinds of symbols.

Another ancient tradition contributed to these works' understanding of the nature of the Torah. This tradition understood the Hebrew alphabet as the material for the creation of the world. This idea was the animating principle of the ancient *Sefer Yeẓirah,* or book of creation. It is reflected in *Tiqqunei ha-Zohar*'s adoption of early kabbalistic linguistic theories.[22] The idea that the Hebrew alphabet houses nascent energies is reflected in the talmudic statement that "Beẓalel [the architect of the Taberbacle] knew how to combine the letters from which heaven and earth were created."[23] According to this tradition, the consonants, the vowels, and the musical notes that accompany the Masoretic text control metaphysical energies.[24] Each of these aspects of the text has a specific power. Sometimes "the vowels are a prophetic voice and the notes of cantillation are weapons"[25] whereas "syllables are contingent on thought, vowels are contingent on speech, and [consonant] letters are contingent on action."[26] The semiotic qualities of the notes are also a factor in their use as images.[27] Individual letters were recognized as having specific qualities.[28] For instance, *Tiqqunei ha-Zohar* contains discourses on the esoteric meaning of the letter *kaf,*[29] the distinction between the letters *dalet* and *resh,*[30] the spatial dimensionality latent in the pontilistic letter *yod,*[31] and the aural qualities of the vowels and notes.[32]

As mentioned previously, certain kabbalistic works, such as Joseph Gikatilla's *Sha'arei Orah,* have a didactic quality in that they instruct the adherent how to make his own analyses of biblical texts. *Tiqqunei ha-Zohar* often adopts the former didactic mode, even utilizing earlier aggadic formulations. One didactic formula employed in the *Tiqqunim* is the early rabbinic exegetical form *ein . . . ella*, "there is none but," meaning "this can mean only." In this way, a phrase such as *ein imo ella Keneset Yisrakel,* which means "his mother can only mean the Community of Israel," goes from being a literal definition of meaning to a quotation from a lost lexicon of kabbalistic symbols.[33] This formula is employed from time to time by the author in reference to a preexistent code for his *kinnuyim,* kabbalistic metaphors and symbols, as in "*his father* means only the Blessed Holy One."[34] Sometimes rabbinic exegetical equations may be adopted, such as "*pegi'ah* (meeting) *is piyusa* (mollification)."[35] Sometimes a specific *kinnui* will have only one meaning.[36] One image may be linked with another in a seamless, flowing free association, as in "*isha* (woman) is *bayit* (house) is a raza *de-Ḥokhmata* (a secret of wisdom)."[37]

Tiqqunei ha-Zohar and *Ra'aya Meheimna* employ a number of traditional Jewish principles of exegetical causality and esoteric meaning, including *gematriyah* (numerical coefficient), *notarikon* (acronym), and *temurah* (permutation). These methods are rife in the works of Abraham Abulafia and especially in the philosophical Kabbalah of Joseph Gikatilla's *Ginnat Egoz,* itself an important source for the author's linguistic formulations. Numerical associations are also commonly adduced, as in "All sevens are from the realm of *Shekhinah*"[38] or "Seven *sefirot,* containing seven names."[39] Punning is also an aspect of this associative play, as in "Four (*revi'i*) facets, which is *ima revi'a 'aleihem* (literally the mother nests on them)."[40] Sometimes the associative flow becomes almost impenetrable, as in "YHHV is a *korban 'oleh ve-yored* (a sliding scale sacrifice), which is *Ima 'Ilaah* (the Transcendent Mother)."[41] In the *Tiqqunim,* these textual minutiae are symbolized, combined, and associated to create what is often a very dense and impenetrable text:

> There is no knowledge like the knowledge of the vowels and cantillation. *Segolta,* of which it says: *Zarka, makaf, shofar, holekh segolta*: All of them are hinted at in *havayim* like this YY"Y HH"H VV"V HH"H, and every place that there are three *yudim* as one, as YYY implies *segolta,* which is the *Shekhinah* that consists of *Ḥokhmah, Ḥesed, Neẓaḥ, Wisdom cries aloud in*

the streets (Proverbs 1:2). So the Masters of the Mishnah maintained: *He who desires wisdom should turn south*[42] for all three are southern. HHH *Binah, Gevurah, Hod,* all of which are to the north, so it says: *He who desires wealth should turn north.*[43]

This text equates the customary order of the notes of cantillation, *Zarka, makaf shofar,* and *segolta,* with the emanative scheme of the Divine name YHVH. The three letters *Yud* are arranged in such a way as to make of the vowel and cantillation point *segolta.* They also symbolize the emanative continuum of the sefirotic tree, the *sefirot Ḥokhmah, Ḥesed, and Neẓaḥ,* on the right side, and *Binah, Gevurah,* and Hod, on the left side.

The narrative structure and meaning of scripture, as well as the semiotic consideration of any of its components, was the source of the contemplative reading that formed the basis of kabbalistic practice. The holiness of the canonical text was always considered as extending into its most inner minutiae.

Kinnui

Kinnui, or "euphemism," originates as a rabbinic legal device, as a term that may be substituted for the name of God as the object of an oath and to prevent inadvertent blasphemy during testimony.[44] The use of this term is largely absent from the sections of the Zohar linked to Moshe de Leon.[45] In *Tiqqunei ha-Zohar* and *Ra'aya Meheimna,* it is the author's central term for symbol or metaphor.

The term *kinnui* had an enduring function in Jewish philosophical literature, particularly at the hands of the Tibbonide translators, who coined much of medieval Hebrew philosophical terminology.[46] In every case, it seems to be used as to mean euphemism, as in this instance in Maimonides' *Guide for the Perplexed:*[47] "All speech that is related to the (Divine) Name may be either a euphemism (*kinnui*) for (Divine) will and desire or a euphemism for that which the name signifies."

In the same way, in Judah ha-Levi's *Kuzari,*[48] the term *kinnui* refers to a situation in which a Hebraism comes to intercede for a Greek philsopical term, as in "perhaps the waters of the act of creation were merely a euphemism (*kinnui*) for the *hiele.*" At the hands of the Tibbonide translators of these philosophical works, a *kinnui* was not a mere translation, but a euphemism that in some way cloaked the original meaning of a term.

Ronald Kiener has noted the presence of this understanding of *kinnui* in his research on the famous Hebrew paraphrase of Sa'adiah Gaon's *Book of Beliefs and Opinions.* This work had an inestimable effect on the developmentof Jewish spirituality in the Middle Ages. As has been noted by Kiener, this remark of the paraphrase to Sa'adiah seems to presage the positions of Joseph Gikatilla and the author of the *Tiqqunim:*[49] "The distinction between the specific names and the euphemistic names is that (the former), such as YH, AHYH, ELOHIM, have no opposite. The *kinuyim,* however, have an opposite such as *Raḥum* (merciful) and its oposite would be *Kanu* (jealous) . . ."

According to the paraphrase of Sa'adiah, the names that have no overt significance are inneffable names, whereas the *kinnuyim* may signify other images. In subsequent Kabbalah, this first catagory of names were called *Havvayin,* in apposition to the *kinnuyim.* A widely known employment of this term is in Joseph Gikatilla's *Sha'arei Orah,* where the various names of God are understood as kinnuyim for the name YHVH:

> (God's) Holy Names mentioned in the Torah are all contingent on the name YHVH. And if you say "Isn't the name AHYH the root and the source?" know that the four-letter name is like the trunk of a tree and the name AHYH is the root of this tree. It takes root there and branches out to all sides. The rest of the Holy Names are like branches and shoots, proceeding out from the trunk, and each of the branches *makes fruit according to its species* (Gen. 1:11). Besides the Holy Name that may not be erased, there are a number of other *kinnuyim* contingent on every name. What are the *kinnuyim* of YHVH? "Full-of-Awe" (*nora*), tolerant of iniquity (*nose 'avon*), passing over sin (*over 'al pesha'*). What are the *kinnuyim* of EL? "Great" (*gadol*) "Compassionate" (*raḥum*) "Gracious" (*ḥanun*). *Kinnuyim* of ELOHIM? "Grand" (*adir*) "Judge" (*shofet*) "Magistrate" (*dayan*). All these *kinnuyim* are other *kinnuyim,*

> contingent on every *kinnui* of these, and they are all the other words of the Torah, till we find that the whole Torah is woven of *kinnuyim* and *kinnuyim* of names, and the holy names are all contingent on the name YHVH; they all unite with it, so that one finds that the whole Torah is woven on the name YHVH, so that it is called (Psalms 19:8) *The Torah, wholly of YHVH.* One must understand the intention of the Holy Names and grasp the specific *kinnuyim* for each of them, trying to cleave to Him, to be in awe and fear of Him, then you will understand the awe of God, and you will find the knowledge of Him . . .[50]

YHVH is the essential name of God, and all of the others have the status of *kinnuyim.* The *kinnuyim* refer to attributes of God, aspects in addition to God's essential nature. The idea of the *kinnui,* therefore, is an extension of Naḥmanides's understanding of the Torah as the names of God, together with the philosophical idea of God being known through the intermediary of the Divine attributes.[51] The author of the *Tiqqunim* was influenced by Gikatilla's use of the *kinnui.* Certainly, it is the most widely employed literary device in the *Tiqqunim* and *Ra'aya Meheima.* In the introduction to the *Tiqqunei ha-Zohar,* the *kinnuyim* are portrayed as independent entities: "the Most Transcendent permitted all the holy names and beings and all the *kinnuyim* to reveal their hidden secrets to [the adepts], every name on its own level, and the ten *sefirot* were permitted to reveal to them hidden secrets that will not be permitted to be revealed until the generation when the Messiah comes."[52]

The *kinnuyim,* like the names of God and the *sefirot* themselves, are aspects of God's incarnate presence. God *permits* the *kinnuyim* to come down and reveal themselves, as if the *kinnuyim* have an independent existence apart from God's will and nature. Just as the *sefirot* are a vessel for the immanence of God, their *kinnuyim* are also vessels for multiplicity of expression. *Havvayin* are all the permutations of the name YHVH, and the *kinnuyim* comprise the remaining symbols and names of God, including ELOHIM,[53] one of the most common biblical appellations for God. This idea is supported by the system of numerical causality, *gematriya.* According to this system, ELOHIM and *kinnui* are equated through their shared numerical value of eighty-six. *Kinnui* signifies a degree of Divinity equivalent to the term ELOHIM, the "God" of subsequent English translation:

> They sanctify God's name above, among the spirits of the other peoples, and every spirit is known by his *kinnui,* but Israel are known above, by the name YHVH that is the life of all *kinnuyim* and every name and *kinnui* witnesses to it. EL witnesses it for it is greater than any people, as in (Job 5:8) *I would resort to EL.* ELOHIM witnesses on it because He is ELOHAY HA-ELOHIM, as ADNY because of ADONAY HA-ADONIM.[54]

The author's free interpretations of biblical texts were mandated and justified through the medium of the *kinnuyim.* The *kinnui,* a product of philosophy and theosophical Kabbalah, was elevated to the importance of the ancient tradition of God's primordial names.

As in *Sha'arei Orah,* the formulation of the *kinnui* in *Tiqqunei ha-Zohar* also seems indebted to medieval speculations regarding the attributes of God. In the *Ra'aya Meheimna,* there is this explanation of the theological function of the *kinnui*:

> One must know that He is called "Wise," with all kinds of wisdom, "Understanding," with all kinds of understanding, "Saintly," with all kinds of saintliness, "Heroic," with all kinds of heroism, "Counsel," with all kinds of counsel, "Righteous," with all kinds of righteousness, and "King," with all kinds of royalty, until infinity. In all these levels, in one He will be called "Compassionate," and in one He will be called "Judge," and so forth on a number of levels until infinity. Certainly there is a distinction between "Compassionate" and "Judge"! Before the world was created, however, He was known by those qualities that had yet to exist, for if there was no world, how could He be the Compassionate Judge?! His qualities were potential. Therefore, all names are His *kinnuyim* because of His actions. He therefore created the soul in His image, to be known through its functions, so that every limb of the body is called a microcosm. The Master of the World does

> this with every creature and in every generation according to its acts. The soul is defined according to the actions of its limbs. A limb that fulfills a commandment causes the soul to be called "compassion," "kindness," "grace," and "mercy," while that limb that commits a transgression, its soul is known as "anger," "judgment," and "rage." It is known apart from the body for its compassion or cruelty. Therefore, the Master of the World created the World and its phenomena. Be they compassionate, or gracious, or judging, His names are *kinnuyim*. He is not called by them, rather every name is a creation of this world. Therefore, when a generation is good, they know Him as YHVH, with the quality of compassion, and when they are sinful, they call Him ADNY[55] with the quality of judgment, according to every generation and individual, but not that He has any particular quality or personal name.[56]

The multiplicity of the *sefirot*, and their *kinnuyim*, describe God's function in the Universe. They do not, however, attempt to describe the unchanging essence that lies at the core of the Divine, at the very height of the sefirotic tree. The *kinnuyim* are a formal application of the medieval theological principle of God's attributes. The sefirotic extensions of the Divine are compared to the limbs of the body. The actions of each describe and often determine the inner nature of the individual. In a formulation similar to Gikatilla's, the name YHVH remains hidden, its corporeal representation transformed by humankind's sinful state. The emanation and interplay of the *sefirot* is described by the *kinnuyim*:

> Each *sefirah* has a personal name and quality and limit and realm. The Master of the World extends through these names, dominates them, is called by them, dwells in them, as the soul dwells in the limbs of the body. As the Master of the World has no personal name, or specific place, but every place is His realm, so the soul has no personal name or place in the body, rather the whole body is its realm, there is no limb empty of it. Therefore, one cannot contain the soul in one place, for then it would be absent in other jurisdictions, nor may one call it by one, two, or three names, to say that it

> is only *Ḥokhmah,* or *Binah,* or *Da'at,* but not more, for that would deny its other aspects. How much more so with the Master of the World, that one must not fix Him in any one place, to call Him by His names . . . [57]

The Jewish philosophical tradition traditionally prized the notion of God's abstraction and ineffability. Symbolization provided a way to express ideas that defied expression in ordinary language. The philosophical doctrine of God's attributes being the closest one may come to the knowledge of God underlay the function of the *kinnuyim.* The attributes of the one God could be multiple, as they were understood as attributes, not the essence of God's unity. Hence, the functions of the *sefirot* could be symbolized in innumerable ways, with the *kinnuyim* being the medium for this expression. In the words of the great systematizer of Zoharic Kabbalah, R. Moshe Cordovero: "The *sefirot* represent various aspects, issues and realities. Every aspect has a name and *kinnui* so that one *kinnui* teaches what another might not.[58]

The *kinnui* signifies the hidden Divinity in the profane world. The oneness of God remains hidden, with the *kinnuyim* representing the function of the Divine in present reality: "for all the *kinnuyim* and all the *Havayim*[59] are *kinnuyim* for Him and He is not a *kinnui."*[60]

Kinnuyim, in the Maimonidean expression, refer to God's actions, not God's ineffable essence. There is a profusion of symbols to represent the divided realm of *Malkhut,* the *sefirah* of present existence. This *sefirah* is the realm of corporeality, the dichotomous realm of the *Shekhinah,* the feminine aspect of the Divine: "The transcendent mother has one *kinnui* that comes out to the sum of ELOHIM, and that *kinnui* is light and darkness."[61]

An important aspect of the author's use of the *kinnuyim* lies in his egalitarian employment of source material. Besides the characteristic tropes of the Hebrew Bible, the *kinnuyim* were apt to include images from the *aggadah,* the homiletics and lore of the Talmud. They also a display a compelling use of halakhic rhetoric and dicta. This alignment of rabbinic materials with motifs from the biblical canon will figure significantly in determining this mystic's attitudes toward rabbinic tradition and authority.

This process is portrayed in terms of the halakhic institution of levirate marriage, in which a man was a required to marry his brother's widow. The ambivalent nature of this institution, with its admixture of joy and sorrow, inspired much kabbalistic interpretation:

> At that time it says of the *Shekhinah* (Deuteronomy 28:9): . . . *and he took off his shoe,* the shoe of the Blessed Holy One to uphold what it says: [take off your shoe and unify with the] *Shekhinah,* which is called *ḥaliẓah,* the *hilluẓ ha-na'al* [taking off the sandal]. They don't have to unite with the world though levirate marriage as it says (Ruth 4:7): . . . *so it is in Israel, a man takes off his shoe and gives it to his neighbor.* The shoe is the *kinnui,* "a locked garden" to opening the lock as in *Sin crouches by the door* (Genesis 4:7), the sin passes and the gate is opened.[62]

In this example, the kabbalistic symbol is the device that obstructs the essence of the Divine. The adept discards the "shoe" that has been thrown in the face of the lesser interpreter of the Divine text. Just as levirate marriage is up to the discretion of the couple, so the decision to accept the oblique meaning or delve into the deeper meaning of the text is up to the reader.

The use of the term *kinnui* in *Tiqqunei ha-Zohar* is significant, as it admits a distinction between a symbol and the meaning that it signifies. *Kinnui* opens the possibilities of kabbalistic creativity to the adept, through its implicit sanction of randomness, multiplicity, and pluralism.[63] According to the principles of this symbolic hermeneutic, a multitude of undeveloped meanings are nascent in the sprawl of the sacred text.

The literature of theosophical Kabbalah was altogether concerned with the interaction of such symbols. The author adopted Joseph Gikatilla's self-conscious use of the *kinnui* and made it the central literary methodology of the *Tiqqun* form. The use of the *kinnui* is important for at least two reasons. First of all, the *Tiqqunim* themselves are literally structured in a profusion of *kinnuyim* linked together. The *Tiqqun* is a celebration of the principle of multiplicity. Beginning each *Tiqqun* with "In the Beginning . . . ," the author builds long homilies based on the interlocking, associative semiotic nature of the *kinnuyim*. The *Tiqqunim* seem to have been composed to convey the mystic's inner state. In so doing, the mystic struggles to part the curtain of symbols to peer, fleetingly, into the essence of the Divine. The mystic follows the path of the associative flow of the *kinnuyim*, as they circle and overlay the hidden essence of reality. The symbols of any mystical or religious tradition evoke the nature of its religious vision and are necessarily infused with elements of mystery and awe. *Kinnui* is the device that hides the essential reality of the divine from all but the cognoscenti.

3

The *Maskilim*: Mystical Vocation in the *Tiqqunim*

Mystics have their experiences in isolation, if only the isolation of their own minds. The inwardness of the mystical experience often removes the mystic from the social structure. If mystics identify with religious structures prior to their experiences, then they can reintegrate into their society, by communicating and propagating the content of their experience. The mystic's isolation and alienation are provisional, then, as the conclusions of his or her experience may lend themselves to social application, perhaps by the mystic's disciples.

This chapter explores the ideas of mystical vocation in the *Tiqqunim* and *Ra'aya Meheimna* and the author's understanding of the mystic's relationship to religious authority. The mystic's social role was defined in contradistinction and sometimes in opposition to the role of the rabbinic legal authority. Although the author of the Zohar contented himself with the creation of an attractive romance of a distant past, *Tiqqunei ha-Zohar* and *Ra'aya Meheimna* chartered a movement with contemporary application.

In *Tiqqunei ha-Zohar* and *Ra'aya Meheimna's* system of religious values, the agent of religious truth is the *maskil* or enlightened mystic. The *maskilim* are an order of mendicant kabbalists, whose charter is the Zohar.[1] The image of a mystical fellowship, whose members wandered the districts of the Galilee, sharing their contemplative visions, had already been portrayed in the Zohar. *Tiqqunei ha-Zohar* and *Ra'aya Meheimna* formalized this role, particularly in terms of the mystic's relationship to society, social authority, and the cosmic order.

The main practice of this mystical order was the contemplation of the Torah in kabbalistic terms. This kind of reading, which derived from the literary nature of rabbinic midrash, was the characteristic literary feature of the Zohar and its related literature. In its chartering of a movement devoted to the practice of symbolic reading, the *maskilim* of *Tiqqunei ha-Zohar* represent the apex and closure of the theosophical Kabbalah, in that the text of the Zohar became canonical, although the creation of new texts of this nature was sanctioned.

The terms *maskil* and *zohar* derive from the verse in Daniel[2] "The enlightened (*maskilim*) will be radiant (*yazhiru*) like the bright expanse of the sky, and those who lead the many to righteousness will be like the stars forever and ever." This phrase is a staple of Zoharic imagery, as the term *will be radiant* is built on the verb *ZHR*, the basis of the word *zohar*. This text forms the basis for the introductory proem of *Tiqqunei ha-Zohar*, and a number of lesser treatments of the text occur in the *Tiqqunei Zohar Ḥadash*.[3] The main sections of the Zohar generally interpreted this text in terms of the dynamics of the emanatory process, particularly the conjunction of the lower *sefirot*: *Yesod* and *Malkhut*.[4] The brightness or shining of the *maskilim*, according to the broadest interpretation of the text, is the hypostatic emanation of Divinity into corporeality through the medium of these *sefirot*.

In the *Midrash ha-Ne'elam*,[5] arguably the earliest stratum of the Zohar, the image *zohar* signifies the soul's descent into the body.[6] Elsewhere, the Zohar portrays *maskilim* as the supporting *sefirot* of the Divine superstructure, "those who contemplate with wisdom all that the Palanquin[7] and her supports require . . . for if it didn't shine on them [i.e. the *maskilim*], they would never be able to perceive it."[8] In this way, the term *maskilim* represents the emanated aspect of the cosmic order, as well as the mystics who contemplate it. The many portrayals of the *maskilim* in the *Tiqqunim* show the mystic using the charged, symbolic reading of the Holy Text as the vehicle for enlightenment. To cite one instance: "*Ha-maskilim*—These are the ones who look at the secret of wisdom, the inner secrets of the Torah—the ones who do the will of their master and who practice the Torah day and night."[9]

Through his mystical reading, the *maskil* becomes a conduit for the flow of the Divine effluence; he is absorbed into the emanation of reality from the Divine mind.[10] This loss of self causes the mystic's consciousness to become a mere instrument for the reception of Divine effluence: "*Ha-maskilim*—They practice the Torah and contemplate the words of the Torah with intention and contemplation. . . . they contemplate, not the word itself, but the place on which that word is contingent. For there is no word that is not contingent on another, higher word. In this word is found the other word, of higher meaning."[11] The symbolized word of the Torah points to a higher reality.

The *maskil* 's contemplative pietism begins with submission to the law, with the embrace of an obedient faith.[12] The self-abnegation required for the acceptance of the "yoke of the Kingdom of Heaven" transforms the mystic into a vessel for the outflow of Divine effluence:

> *Maskilim*—who contemplate the secret of wisdom, the inner secrets of the Torah, these are the *ẓaddikim* who do the will of the Master and practice the Torah day and night, these are the *maskilim*, knowing the will of the Master best. Have we not learned that there is no level like their level, so that those who practice the Torah are called *maskilim*, who contemplate with wisdom, with the secret of higher wisdom? The Infinite [*Ein Sof*] sends out its hidden, unknown light, proceeding from *Ein Sof*, through the supports, and the *maskilim*, who know the secret of secrets, contemplate, illuminated by that flowing brightness. Sustaining the secrets of the Torah, they know how to contemplate its hiddenness. . .[9]

In at least one instance, the Zohar interprets *maskilim* as a metaphor for the notes of cantillation.[14] *Tiqqunei ha-Zohar* expands this idea to mean that enlightenment descends through the medium of the cantillation,[15] as well as through the letters[16] and the vowels of the Torah text.[17] Although the cantillation, vocalization, and inflection are intoned by the reader, they include a transpersonal dimension. The gnosis of the exegetical moment makes the *maskil* one with the text and its unfolding of meaning.

The *maskil* aspires to the consciousness of the greatest biblical heroes and talmudic sages. The Zohar itself presaged this use of the term *maskilim* by juxtaposing them with the biblical Patriarchs themselves: "Did the Patriarchs not know? Rather, the *maskilim,* who are these? The wise, who *themselves* contemplate things that people cannot say with their mouths,[18] these are called *maskilim.*"[19]

Tiqqunei ha-Zohar repeatedly equates the *maskil's* dreams and visions with prophecy.[20] The prophecy attainable through symbolic reading is nothing but the direct apprehension of the immanence of God: "When the Blessed Holy One draws forth prophecy, all the *sefirot* are unified."[21] Prophecy exists, *in potentia,* in the nature of the symbolic text.[22] The *maskil's* quest for gnosis conforms to the classical rabbinical typologies of prophetic experience. The highest level is represented by the lucid speculum of Moses' prophecy.[23] The lowest level of perception is the clouded glass, the instrument of the *Sitra Aḥra,* the demonic force of separation and distension:[24] "*He who is adept* [*maskil*] *in a matter* [*davar*][25] *will attain success* (Proverbs 16:20). *Davar* is the clouded mirror . . . *will attain success* is the clear mirror. [It is written] *adept on a matter* and not *in* a matter, for he must look at that which is above, the shining firmament (*zohar ha-raqi'a*). From that firmament he could glimpse the shining that shines from the primordial point, that shines and flashes with other lights."[26]

The mystic's intellect is the agency of the mystical ascent and union, not his theurgic practices or meditative techniques. The spiritual claims of this contemplative spirituality were later defined by R. Moshe Cordovero in the following terms: "it is a functional spirituality, which facilitates vision. Through it, one perceives and has great vision. This angelic apperception is superior to our perception, like the vision of the mind over that of the eye.[27] . . . This is the vision of contemplation, when one sees the future and the past, and from the subtlety of his intellect he understands."[28]

Gershom Scholem also portrayed the nuances of this charged, symbolic perception of esoteric reality in this way:

> All creation, from the world of the highest angel to the lower realms of physical nature, refers symbolically to the law which operates within it—the law which governs the world of the *sefirot.* In everything something is reflected . . . from the realms which lie in the center of it. Everything is transparent, and in this state of transparency everything takes on a symbolic character. This means that everything, beyond its own meaning, has something more, something which is part of that which shines into it or, as if in some devious way, that which has left its mark behind in it, forever . . .[29]

In sefirotic terms, the *maskil's* enlightenment comes as a result of the linking of the *sefirah* of *Binah,* the receptacle for the more ineffable *sefirot,* with the corporeal realm of *Shekhinah,*[30] through the realms of *Malkhut* [31] and *Tif'eret.*[32] *Shekhinah is* a metaphor for the nature of the transcendent and the ineffable as well as the vicissitudes of the soul in the body.[33] Enlightenment comes about through the classical erotic metaphor of *hieros gamos* employed so widely in the theosophical Kabbalah. In the words of the *Tiqqunim*: "The *maskilim* have the wisdom to know the daughter's ascent in prayer, through the letters, vowels, and cantillation, to raise love and peace and union and intimacy between them through their qualities, to unify them as one[34] . . . Masters of Torah, from the realm of the central pillar, in which at midnight King David arose[35] to unite with the *Shekhinah* (who is night)" . . .[36]

As intercessors between the text and its esoteric meaning, the *maskilim* are like *shadkhanim,* or matchmakers, brokering the union of the adherent with the Divine. The *Tiqqunim* and Zohar both employ various images of intercession in their portrayal of the *maskilim.* The mystics intervene between the highest levels of the transcendent and the prosaic dimension of present reality, through their mystical understanding of the Torah.

The Zohar as Mystical Charter

Tiqqunei ha-Zohar and *Ra'aya Meheimna* present the Zohar as the central charter and instrument of their mystical order. These works are among the first exegeses of the Zohar and also form the basis for subsequent Zohar commentaries. According to the author's understanding, the *maskil* was guided by the Zohar and also committed to the expansion and exegesis of that vast work. The *maskilim* are often juxtaposed with the author's invocation of Zohar as the charter of his contemporary mystical vocation: "The *maskilim* understand from the realm of *Binah*, the Tree of Life, through your composition that is the *Sefer ha-Zohar*, from the shining of the higher mother, which is repentance, for in the future Israel will taste from this Tree of Life that is this book *Zohar*."[37]

The Israeli historian Yiẓḥak Baer was interested in tracing the relationship between the author of the *Ra'aya Meheimna* and Christian pietistic circles in Castile. Baer saw the author's use of the Zohar as similar to Christian pietist's use of manuals of behavior in their orders. "It is as if the Zohar is thought of as a book of daily practice (or even as an actual book of decrees)—a kind of covenantal book for a circle of initiates, functioning, like the Franciscans, and receiving into their circle others who are prepared to assume their ascetic stringencies, or at least to keep the commandments of the Torah."[38]

In making this comparison, Baer erred in his portrayal of the Zoharic literature. The Zohar could hardly be an efficient manual of practice, because of the extended novel form that characterizes much of its composition. Only certain parts of the Zohar—for instance, the sections called *Piqqudim* and *Matnitin*—adhere to the format of *sifrei miẓvot* or "books of commandments." The *Ra'aya Meheimna*, with its emphasis on the Temple cult, is hardly a manual of discipline for a medieval author. It is more plausible to assume that the Zohar was understood as a sacred text for the purposes of the adept's mystical contemplation. This would explain the preeminence of texts such as the *Idrot*, which detail, in a systematic fashion, the supernal secrets of the Godhead.

In sefirotic terms, the Zohar mediates the relationship between the Tree of Life, that is, the upper *sefirot* and the Tree of Knowledge, the realm of prosaic existence.[39] The *maskilim* are the incarnate reflection of the heavenly pantheon. The Zohar intercedes between the angels above and the mystical scholars below:

> The *maskilim* are the 600,000 Masters of the Mishnah above. There are 600,00 Masters of the Mishnah below; these are the 600,000 angels and these 600,000 stars shine as it says:[40] *Moses' face was like the face of the Sun. They will shine* in its words, they will all shine in its writing in this book, *Like the shining of the firmament,* in whose name it is called the book *Zohar* (shining), in the image of the inner pillar that is *Sefer* (book). Its brightness comes from the middle pillar that is *SFR*. Its brightness comes from the Great Mother that is *Zohar,* therefore the Rabbis said: *Who is wise?*[41] *He who understands the inner meaning.* This is the Zohar that shines in the heart of the Faithful Shepherd, the brightness[42] of the thirty-two instances of ELOHIM in the act of creation.[43]

Tiqqunei ha-Zohar saw the Zohar itself, like the Torah, as consisting of fragmented letters, each with a higher secret.[44] The Zohar itself was seen as having the numinosity of any other sacred text in the biblical and rabbinic canon. This understanding helped to expedite the Zohar's own passage into canonic status and its incorporation into the liturgy. When the *Tiqqunim* and *Ra'aya Meheimna* were published with the printed texts of the Zohar, they became part of the Zoharic canon and, by association, the Jewish canon. The Zohar literature, as a whole, came to self-consciously portray its own sacredness, creating a kind of historical closure to the classical period of theosophical Kabbalah.

Piety and Poverty

The essential behavior and conduct of the *maskil* follow the contours of the most classical acts of Jewish piety. The esoteric dimension of this piety is built on classic rabbinic values of humility and self-abnegation, to the point of immolation.[45] This piety also draws on the rabbinic understanding of the nature of Torah study. In the Zohar and *Tiqqunim*, study is seen as an ascent to the realm of Divine thought.[46] The Zohar naturally used the classical typologies of Jewish piety, as it claimed to depict the spiritual life of the *tannaim*. *Tiqqunei ha-Zohar* and *Ra'aya Meheima* continued the use of these typologies in the portrayal of the *maskil*.[47]

The Zohar understands the religious saint, or *ẓaddik*, as God's intermediary. The *ẓaddik* intercedes between God and humankind. The *ẓaddik's* leadership redeems the people, and he or she feels the people's pain acutely. The *ẓaddik's* intercession is not through the monistic manipulation of impersonal forces. The *ẓaddik* is, rather, a third party and buffer in the dynamics of the personal relationship between God and the people Israel.[48]

An important literary motif in the Zohar is that of the elevation of the societally marginal. Commonly, a member of some humble stratum of society is revealed as a secret purveyor of hidden wisdom hiding the magnitude of his or her spirituality. Enlightenment is apt to come from an infant, a donkey driver, or an apparently addled old man. This literary motif carries explicit criticism of the frequent obtuseness of rabbinic authority. It is common for the Zohar to portray the figure of the pauper, who "has nothing of his own,"[49] as symbolic of *Malkhut*, the *sefirah* of present existence, which is merely a receptacle for the influxes of the other *sefirot*.[50] It is clear that, based on the foundation laid by the Zohar, the *maskil* requires no societal approbation.

The potential of this nascent literary motif is realized in the *Ra'aya Meheimna* and *Tiqqunim*, which speak of the spiritual value of poverty and self-abnegation for the sake of the Torah.[51] *Tiqqunei ha-Zohar* and *Ra'aya Meheimna* see this value as latent in a number of rabbinic dicta, such as *There is no poverty besides that of Torah* [52] and *You shall love the Lord with all your soul, even if he takes your soul,*[53] and *Poverty is a kind of death.*[54] The travail of poverty is "like the seven fires of *Geihinnom*,"[55] but, nonetheless, the mystic "gives God what he loves best."[56]

Poverty is not an ideal state, but is, rather, the fault of society. *Ra'aya Meheimna*, in particular, expresses dissatisfaction with societal and religious values. The author is scornful of those burghers who are reluctant to support the mendicant scholars of the community: "The miser and his money are disgraceful! Because he doesn't contribute, he is not from the seed of the patriarchs . . . because he does not benefit the masters of the Torah, by supporting them."[57]

Yiẓḥak Baer and Isaiah Tishby disputed whether poverty is a necessary part of *Ra'aya Meheimna*'s mystical system. It was Baer's contention[58] that poverty was a goal and religious value. Baer thought that this implied a positive value in suffering and considered this to be another indication of the author's contact with Joachide pietism, which valued poverty and renunciation. According to Baer: "Our cabalist author lists poverty as one of the characteristics of Messianic times. It is not, as the Talmud sees it, one of the final tribulations of Messianic travail, but rather a religious end in itself. Poverty is a means of sanctification voluntarily assumed. It is a becoming trait, not only of the people to-be-redeemed and of its redeemer, but of the Divinity itself. Here is a case of a tradition turning Dogma."[59]

Contradicting this view, Isaiah Tishby[60] pointed out that the main sections of the Zohar generally extol the virtues of the poor alongside of the virtue of charity, albeit from a position of *noblesse oblige*. According to Tishby, the author of the *Tiqqunim* accepts the suffering of the poor *ẓaddik* but does not make a specific, desirable virtue of poverty. The mystic's benighted state is as perverse and unfair as the benighted state of the people Israel. According to Tishby: "The poor *Shekhinah* and Moses don't glorify their poverty, rather they complain of their suffering and degradation."[61] Persuasively, he argues that "this is not a tradition of holy poverty, only of holy paupers."[62] Certainly, Baer's argument for a Judaic "vow of poverty" would support his thesis that there was considerable contact between theosophical kabbalists and the Franciscan and Joachide pietists of Castile. Tishby's understanding seems the more plausible: that poverty is a condition that may accompany the mystics's condition, but is not necessarily an inevitable precondition for mystical practice.

The most recent published remarks on this issue are also the most definitive. A contemporary authority on the *Tiqqunim* and *Ra'aya Meheimna*, Amos Goldreich,[63] has written:

> This sharp motif is perhaps the acme of the theological structures of the *Tiqqunei ha-Zohar* literature that deal with the sources of poverty, which churned in the depths of the author's soul: classes of wealthy, powerful, and parsimonious Jews, at whose hand our author suffered no little bit. This can only be the personal fate of the author, drawn into a metahistorical vision, whose roots are based in the conflict between the Divine and demonic forces. As opposed to the Zohar, which has so much vital interest in the demonic and its array of forces (apparently from the traditions of the Castilean kabbalists, as well as the author's own tendencies toward the realm of myth), the author of *Tiqqunei ha-Zohar* was not so interested in metaphysical evil, but rather in its concrete historical and societal manifestations.

Goldreich's distinction between the preoccupations of the Zohar and the *Tiqqunim* is particularly apt. In sefirotic terms, the *Ra'aya Meheimna*'s main interest is with *Malkhut*, the *sefirah* of present existence. For instance, the Zohar often presents the Messiah, a paradigm of *Malkhut*, as a pauper. This understanding provides an opportunity for the author to equate poverty with the presence of the *sefirah* of *Malkhut*. The mystic's suffering also derives from his heightened identification with the suffering of the *Shekhinah*, the other great paradigm of *Malkhut*. *Metatron*, the demiurgic angel, is portrayed bewailing the lot of the righteous: "Wherever the sages cast their eyes there is either poverty or death. These are the maidens who die young, all of them are under my jurisdiction in the celestial academy. Why is this? Because the *Shekhinah* is among them . . ."[64]

The depth of the author's preoccupation with the phenomenon of poverty is reflected in his symbolic interpretation of rabbinic ethical dicta. The Mishnah's well-known injunction, "He who uses the crown will depart" (*de-ishtammash betaga ḥalaf*),[65] relates particularly to the dilemma of the poor adept. According to kabbalistic metaphysics, the aspects of

Shekhinah in all the *sefirot* come from *Keter*, the crown (Aramaic, *taga*), but this aspect is transformed (*ḥalaf*) in the process of immanence.[66] The delicate crowns on the Torah text indicate the Torah's origins in the ineffable, as they are made up of the faintest possible markings on the scroll's parchment.[67] Using the "crown" profanes the delicate interaction between *Malkhut* and *Yesod* and throws the transformative moment into the realm of the demonic *qelippot*.[68] This is really a kind of double metaphor, as the crown may also be the crown of the *sefirah Yesod*, at the apex of *Malkhut*. The sexual connotation of the term *ishtammash* reinforces the Zohar's erotic metaphor for mystical union.[69]

A further understanding of *de-ishtammash be-taga ḥalaf* derives from a talmudic reinterpretation associated with R. Shimon ben Lakish,[70] in which the illicit use of the crown refers to the act of passing the secrets to one who is not worthy[71] or deriving gain from teaching the Law.[72] The mystic's merit, accrued through his pietistic practice, is not for his own benefit. These energies are reserved for the needs of the community; selfish use of them is compared to using the property of orphans.[73] The Torah is the instrument of redemption,[74] but its practitioners immolate themselves through their practice. Therefore "there is no real poverty except of Torah,"[75] and the mystic is counseled to remain stoic in the face of his suffering.

Similarly, the injunction against practicing the *miẓvot al menat le-qabel peras*, that is, "for the sake of a reward,"[76] has a metaphysical dimension. The act of claiming a reward is a mark of enslavement to the demonic.[77] It is therefore a betrayal of the adept's royal birthright: his relationship to the Messiah.[78] The most appropriate model of humility is that of a child honoring his or her parents.[79]

The mendicant pietist's lot is the alienation of exile: wandering and rootlessness.[80] This dynamism of change is expressed through various halakhic actions of change: changing one's name, one's location, and on the Sabbath, one's actions. This restlessness is also evoked by the author's use of biblical literary motifs. The patriarchs of Genesis or the dove of the flood account[81] are exemplars of the redemptive nature of wandering and rootlessness.

The *maskil's* life-style is painful. His extra measure of knowledge is a particular burden because he is unrecognized by the community, whose attentions belong to the courtiers and demagogues whose philosophical allegiances are anathema to him. The mystic's true dilemma is that he is socially ineffectual in a world beset by interactions of mythic forces whose real nature only he knows. So it is that loneliness, dependency, and exile are the price the mystic pays for the gnosis of kabbalistic wisdom.

4

The Myth of Chaos

> To identify for a given writer the state from which Adam fell is to reconstruct the writer's concept of the ideal human being and the ideal human condition. This ideal will be found to be all pervasive in that writer's thought system. Thus, the messianic period will be viewed as a restoration of Adam's condition before the Fall, and for the period between the beginning and the End—the here and now—a program will be conceived to retrieve the lost ideal. At a minimum, such a scheme provides a helpful perspective on a writer. At best, it may provide the key to his thought.[1]

In the *Tiqqunim* and *Ra'aya Meheimna,* present existence is suffused with qualities of exile and loss. The *maskil* understands that the world is enmeshed in an ontology of chaos. The mystic's loneliness and alienation result from his heightened sensitivity to this truth. This alienation is expressed in myths of prehistory and exile, derived from the author's selection of mythic *aggadot.*

The Talmud and *midrashim* are heterogeneous anthologies of multiple sources, culled over a period of several centuries. If they manifest a unifying mentality, it is that of the compiler and final editor. Zoharic texts, on the other hand, resemble late and medieval *midrashim* in that they are distinguished by the unifying perspective of a single author. In the Zohar, the author's voice asserts itself in his selection and interpretation of the midrashic canon. Narratives from the *midrash* are combined and reconstructed into a coherent myth. This recurring myth haunts the kabbalistic author's thinking as he constructs a world-view based on primordial traditions of rabbinic esotericism. These traditions might be remnants of a lost rabbinic esotericism. The utilization of these early legends constitutes a particularly "received" aspect of the theosophic Kabbalah, in that the term *kabbalah* means "received tradition."

Although *Tiqqunei ha-Zohar* clearly builds on the Zohar's assemblage of source material, the author nevertheless incorporates aggadic motifs that the Zohar omits or does not explore. These motifs are recombined in such a way as to present a unified myth of prehistory and its relation to the present. Humankind's present dilemmas derive from these mythic events. The events of Genesis, then, are not confined to remote history, but continue to unfold in the present.

The Zohar perceives the dilemmas of humankind as deriving, at least in part, from the consequences of the fall of Adam. The kabbalistic uses of the mythos of the fall reveal the tension between two great extraneous influences: Neoplatonic optimism and gnostic pessimism. Hence, the tradition of Adam as the primordial man probably has its origins in the mysterious relationship between early Kabbalah and Manicheanism, Catharism, and other esoteric traditions that were presumably within the kabbalists' intellectual orbit.[2] Both the Zohar and the *Tiqqunim* cite the midrashic tradition that God created a number of prior worlds, and was later compelled to destroy them (*boneh 'olamot u-maḥarivan*).[3] The present world was created through the emanation of the Divine effluence through the *sefirot*.

The tensions and rivalries of those previous worlds continue into contemporary history. Biblical figures confront one another again, renewed through the principle of *gilgul* or transmigration, particularly among the Edenic generations,[4] and the lineages around Moses.[5] The fall was important to *Tiqqunei ha-Zohar* and *Ra'aya Meheimna,* for it began a chain of catastrophes that continue to unfold, defining the fallen condition of existence. Focal points for the author's portrayal of the fall were its themes of seduction, the power of evil, and the role of the demonic in present existence.

Traditions of the seduction and defilement of Eve by the serpent originate in a number of classical Rabbinic sources. One talmudic tradition portrays the serpent as having implanted *zohama* (impurity) in Eve.[6] This tradition recurs in theosophical Kabbalah, particularly in the *Bahir*,[7] the Zohar,[8] and the *Tiqqunim*.[9] In the *Tiqqunim*, the serpent is a paradigm of deceit,[10] an agent of the *sefirah* of *Din*, harsh judgment.[11] The banishment from the Garden of Eden continues into the present, for "the serpent is the promiscuous woman who destroys the *Shekhinah* by separating her from her husband."[12] In sefirotic terms, the tradition of seduction and implantation implies a defilement in the *sefirah Malkhut*, caused by the illicit union of the serpent and Eve. The implantation of evil in Eve is not only impregnation, it also implies a demonic aspect in womankind, as well as a demonic strain in the primordial geneologies. Hence, present reality is an admixture of good and evil. It is the adept's task to attain the former and overcome or eliminate the latter.

The fall is depicted as an entrance into the realm of *qelippah*, the demonic husk that acts as a barrier to the Holy. According to one rabbinic tradition, Adam "stretched his foreskin" and thereby brought sexual transgression into the world.[13] The term, "stretched his foreskin" (*mashakh be-'orlato*) originally referred to episplasm, the practice by which Hellenized Jews sought to cover the evidence of their circumcisions. The Zohar[14] and *Tiqqunim*[15] understand this expression as a withdrawal into the realm of the demonic *qelippah*. Subsequent Kabbalah equated the profanation of the covenant with masturbation, although not specifically in this case.[16] In the words of the Zohar, "He separated the holy covenant from its place and its portion, truly he stretched his foreskin, discarded the holy covenant, cleaved to his foreskin and was seduced by the word of the serpent."[17]

The sexual aspect of the fall forced Adam into the realm of the demonic, symbolized by the foreskin. In one of the longer treatments of this theme, alchemical motifs dealing with the smelting of metals are used to portray the continuing effects of the fall through subsequent generations:

> Come and see, when the pure Adam was clothed in Abraham, he was whitened by it. In Isaac he was smelted as it says . . . *I will smelt them as one smelts silver and test them as one tests gold* (Zechariah 13:9). In Jacob he sees his image and reproduces. How so? For the Good Inclination (*yeẓer ha-tov*) and the Evil Inclination (*yeẓer ha-ra*), which are the good *Adam* and the evil *Adam,* the Blessed Holy One provided three commandments: idolatry, lewdness and bloodshed . . . [18]

Before the fall, Adam embodied the good and evil inclinations, the impulse to goodness and the impulse to sin. The Evil Inclination is portrayed as an incarnate demonic spirit, and the catastrophe of the fall is the result of this spirit's malevolence:

> After the Evil Inclination transgressed the commandment of the Blessed Holy One, death was decreed upon him. He said "what will happen if I die? He will merely take another servant!" For the Evil Inclination is a servant, and his wife is a maidservant, and his place would be inherited by another servant. What did he do? He and his wife went to seduce Adam and his wife, who were from the realm of goodness. The wife of the Evil Inclination, Lilit, seduced Adam of the Good Inclination, therefore it says: *The women that you put at my side, she gave me of the tree . . .* (Genesis 3:12) And the Evil Inclination seduced Eve, causing them death, so the Blessed Holy One stripped the Good Inclination from Adam's body in the Garden of Eden and the garments of him and his wife, as it says: *And they perceived that they were naked* (Genesis 3:7) and he expelled them from the Garden, as it says: *He drove Adam out* (Genesis 3:24) and his mate with him. And he brought them down to the seven lands that are valley, cloud, ruin, land, soil, earth, world.[19] He cried out and ascended.[20] Nonetheless, he was naked, unclothed, he and his wife.[21]

The Evil Inclination is a fallen angel, whose tragedy dates from prehistory. Another midrashic figure, Lilit, the queen of the demons and *doyenne* of crib death and nocturnal emission, acts as the Evil Inclination's consort. The generations of the patriarchs are an attempt to restore the unsullied nature of Adam before the fall:

> What did the Blessed Holy One do? He reincarnated him as Abraham, and his wife as Sarah. They brought forth impure progeny, Ishmael, the uncleanliness that the snake implanted in Eve. The Blessed Holy One tempered him in a smelting pot of silver, which was mixed with lead and more lead. When he passed him through the fire, the silver was tempered, whitened, and the residue was taken out, this is the tempering of Adam in Abraham. And the impurity was taken out, this is Ishmael, the impurity that the serpent implanted in Eve. And the reincarnation of Eve, Adam's spouse, glowed red in the fire, releasing the impurities and this was Esau, his redness like the blood of slaughter. Since the feminine came through Isaac, the left is called the feminine. Afterward they both emerged in Jacob and his spouse, his seed and his exile is the surrounding pallor. This is, therefore, the meaning of (Job 33:29): *All these things has God done twice, thrice with a man . . .* [22]

The initial generations of covenantal history are devoted to an attempt to correct the fallen state of humankind through the refinement of the Jewish nation's genealogical line. At the same time, the nations that surround the people Israel are made up of the residue of the refining process, implying that the gentile nations contain, genetically, traces of the demonic.

In pure kabbalistic terms, Adam's sin is understood as taking place in the "mind" of the Divine infrastructure, that is, in the first and second *sefirot*.[23] Such an understanding implies that there is a hierarchical set of values in the sefirotic tree. Defilement at a higher level is more serious because it is more intrinsic, affecting the Divine effluence closer to its source. The extent of the sin is debated, in the *Tiqqunim*, by the members of the celestial academy:

> *Yud* is thought, the place where Adam and Abel sinned. *Aleph* is *Keter Elyon*, *Yud* is thought. This sin rose ever upward. R.

> Eliezer said [to R. Shimon]: "Father, aren't there several thoughts? *Shekhinah* is called thought, and it is the *Yud* from ADNY, *Hokhmah* is thought [*maḥshavah*] and *Keter* is *Aleph* from ADNY . . . and there are several *maḥshavot* [thoughts], this above that. As it says: *For one high official is protected by a higher one and both of them by still higher ones* (Ecclesiastes 5:7) and above all of them is the highest, most hidden thought. How many thoughts are there, clothing one another! Clearly Adam only sinned in the thought that is the garment. As it says: *I was afraid because I was naked, so I hid* (Genesis 3:10). It says of Adam: *I hid* and it says of Moses: *Moses hid his face* (Exodus 3:6).[24]

In this text, Rabbi Eliezer, the son of Rabbi Shimon Bar Yoḥai, confines the scope of the sin to the *sefirah Malkhut*. He attempts to qualify the scope of the fall by attempting to obscure the anthropomorphism of Adam's sinning in the upper *sefirot*. These *sefirot* are, bluntly, the "mind" of God, being at the head of the anthropos formed by the sefirotic tree. Rabbi Shimon responds by emphasizing the encompassing scope of the sin and the fall, comparing it to Moses' brazenness following the incident of the golden calf:

> R. Shimon said, "My son, Certainly Adam sinned in all of them, in the thought that is the garment and in the inner thought. Therefore, when Moses said: *Show me your glory* (Exodus 33:18), He said: "*For no man shall see me and live*" for if he merits to see Me, he will live forever. Therefore he said to him: *You cannot see my face* (Exodus 33:20). For there are no countenances here, only unseen countenances. In the place that *'Ilat ha-'Ilot* is known, in the place that He is revealed, the sin of Adam caused Moses to be unable to gaze upon Him, let alone another. For *'Ilat ha-'Ilot* [25] has fled from the thought in which Adam sinned. Therefore it says: *I was afraid because I was naked, so I hid.*[26]

R. Eliezer seems to concede that the sin was of such magnitude that it had repercussions in Moses' spiritual possibilities. Nonetheless, he insists that the sin ruptured only the secondary *sefirah Ḥokhmah*. Essentially he is arguing for the ultimate transcendence and abstraction in God, a principle clearly derived from philosophical rationalism. Rabbi Shimon's prevailing argument for the accessibility of *'Ilat ha-'Ilot*, the most "potential" and infinite aspects of God, is a victory of mystical antirationalism over Aristotelean rationalism:

> R. Eliezer said: "It is nonetheless clear that he did not sin in the higher thought, rather in that which is the garment, and he remained outside in the intellect without the skull. Therefore *I was afraid*. He trembled from that which was within the inner thought *'Ilat ha-'Ilot*." R. Shimon said to him, "My son, he even sinned in the inner thought, the intellect, from whence comes the seed. It is the flowing of the Tree of Life, the primordial, pure and purified light, three drops of which are implied in the higher *Yud*, with its upper, lower, and middle hook. He mixed their darkness, which separates *'Ilat ha-'Ilot* from the hidden intellect. Therefore, *for no man shall see me and live*, until that very darkness passes away, the inner meaning of *Your sins have made him turn his face away and refuse to hear you* (Isaiah 59:2). For no thought, or eye, can perceive that darkness, till it passes. It is like the lower clouds, of which it says: *Your shelter is in the cloud* (Leviticus 3:44). R. Eliezer and all the fellows and elders of the academy trembled and said, "until now we had not known that the sin was at such a high level!"[27]

Adam sins against his own consciousness through his eating the fruit; he sullies the abstract transcendence of *'Ilat ha-'Ilot* with the divisions and mundane corporeality of the lower *sefirot*. This act, in turn, flaws the potential for human perception of the Divine. The action is truly theurgic, as humankind influences the Divine, and validates theurgic kabbalistic responses to the effects of the fall. This understanding remains faithful to the essential meaning of the text in Genesis, in that Adam and Eve attempt to "become as gods," to attain a Divine level of consciousness.

In response to this transgression, God withdraws from the first two *sefirot*, creating a "garment," or obstacle, between the ineffable and its emanation into the corporeal realm. This same sin was the archetypal gnostic "cutting of the shoots" (*kiẓẓuẓ ba-netiyot*), a rupture in the processes of the Divine flow,[28] in that God withdrew from the workings of the lower *sefirot*, those closer to the functions of humankind. This rupture, Adam's mixing of the "darkness" into the purity of the higher *sefirot*, sets in play the chaotic struggle of the holy and the demonic, a central part of the world-view of the *Tiqqunim* and *Ra'aya Meheimna*.

The World Trees

The metaphysical catastrophe of the fall influences history in a number of ways. *Tiqqunei ha-Zohar* portrays the trees of the Garden of Eden, the *Eẓ Ḥayyim*, the "Tree of Life," and the *Eẓ ha-Da'at Tov va-Ra*, the "Tree of the Knowledge of Good and Evil," as agents of two aspects of Divinity. Since the inception of theosophical Kabbalah, these World Trees have been understood as representing the realms of the prosaic and the transcendent.

The Tree of Life represents the union of the six intermediate *sefirot*. It is an idealized realm of unity, untroubled by the divisions that afflict the lowest *sefirah Malkhut*. It "has no difficulty from the realm of evil, no dispute from the unclean spirit."[29] According to the *Tiqqunim*, mystical teachings are the doctrine of the Tree of Life, whereas *halakhah*, the legal infrastructure, is the doctrine of the Tree of Knowledge.[30] The Tree of Life represents the idealized Torah. Mundane, corporeal existence was manifestly the realm of the Tree of Knowledge; it was the author's expectation that the adept would seek the empowerment that comes from the Tree of Life.[31]

These ideas are used in many ways to interpret the biblical tradition. Eve's secondary position in her relationship with Adam indicates that she existed only on the level of the Tree of Knowledge.[32] Historically, the first tablets that Moses received at Sinai came from the Tree of Life, but the subsequent tablets, bestowed after the incident of the golden calf, came from the Tree of Knowledge.[33]

The Temple service, in particular, invokes the Tree of Life's imagery. The sacrifice's immolation on the altar and the consumption of oil by the Temple candelabrum (itself a symbolic tree) represent the ascent of corporeal energies into the ineffable nature of God.[34] The High Priest's worship on the Day of Atonement, the holiest day of the year, is an ascent into the realm of the Tree of Life: "The Day of Atonement . . . is ruled by the Tree of Life, which has no accuser (*satan*) or affliction. From its realm *evil cannot abide with You* (Psalms 5:5). So the servants rest in the Tree of Life, through it they go free . . . "[35]

The Tree of Knowledge alludes to the Oral Torah, the rituals and practices in present existence,[36] the domain of non-kabbalists.[37] These rituals' function is to alter, correct, and compensate for the deficiencies of the present realm. This is accomplished through performance and observance of the precepts of the law: "All the *miẓvot* hang on the tree, some from the branches, some from the roots, some from the trunk. The Torah is called the Tree of Life, whoever eats from it lives forever. There is also a lower tree, whose branches and roots are all the elixir of death, Samael. Whoever transgresses the Torah is nourished and sustained by that tree. As it says: *On the day you eat from it you will surely die* (Genesis 2:17). From it comes all of life's pain."[38]

The Tree of Life represents a realm of unity, whereas the Tree of Knowledge governs a realm of dichotomy and dualism.[39] "It is half sweet, from the right side, and half bitter, from the left side."[40] The ambivalent nature of this tree is represented by a number of halakhic concepts that have a demonic aspect: the mixed multitude (*'erev rav*) of the Exodus account and the public thoroughfare (*reshut ha-rabbim*) that symbolizes the alienation of exile.[41] The Tree of Knowledge governs the realms of secularism and mundanity:

> The Tree of Knowledge rules the weekdays, the Adam of the good and evil impulses[42] as it is written: And the *Lord God formed*[43] *Adam* (Genesis 2:7). It is the Tree of Good and Evil with which Adam sinned. This is Metatron, the servant, ruling the six tractates of the Mishnah, the physical realm, and he presides over the six days of the week, which are either profane or pure, and from it are brought the six tractates of the Mishnah, forbidden and permitted, impure and pure, fit or unfit, in it is *Six days shall you labor and do all your work* and there is no labor but prayer.[44]

If its nature is misinterpreted, the Tree of Knowledge is potentially demonic. It may block or negate higher dimensions of knowledge. In the words of Yiẓḥak Baer: "The bitter waters of the Tree of the knowledge of Good and Evil are euphemisms for secularism, wealth, and other pleasures of the flesh and to the sophistic wisdom of the philosophical theologians, so heuristic and excessive in their talmudic casuistry."[45]

The qualities of division and dialectic that characterize rabbinic scholasticism originate in the duality of this tree: "The Tree of Knowledge requires distinction between the good and evil, just as God distinguished between light and darkness. And one must prune[46] so that the individual can be without evil inclination, and King David cut it away and killed it with his learning."[47]

Rabbinic images of trees are employed as metaphors for the World Trees. *Tiqqunei ha-Zohar* invokes the universal symbol of the master and community as a tree with spreading branches and strong roots relates directly to these World Trees.[48] The classical image of gnostic heresy, "cutting the shoots," *kiẓuẓ ba-netiyot,* is a break in the contiguity of the two trees.[49]

The author of the *Tiqqunim* cites the rabbinic injunction that the practitioner be *tokho ke-varo,* "identical internally and externally." In plain terms, this stricture implies that a religious personality requires consistency, a social injunction that is here reinterpreted in metaphysical terms. *Tokho ke-varo* is interpreted as a portrayal, on the part of the mystic, of the interlocking and overlapping of the Tree of Life and the Tree of Knowledge:

> He is from the Tree of Good and Evil, for he says one thing in his heart and another in his mouth. Who is from the Tree of Life? He who is consistent, internally and externally, mouth and heart equal, about which it says: *He should . . . take from the Tree of Life and live forever.* Of the other, who is not consistent, whose mouth and heart are not the same, it says: *But as for the Tree of Knowledge of Good and Evil, you must not eat from it* (Genesis 2:7). For this is the evil mixing of silver and lead that counterfeits the King's coinage, as in the sin of Eve, when the serpent planted his uncleanliness in her . . .

In this way the talmudic injunction, "Anyone who is not *tokho ke-varo* shouldn't come to the study house,"[51] is amplified by the understanding that *tokho ke-varo* really means "that what is within all the worlds is the same as that which is without . . ."[52] The adept must be spiritually integrated to gain entry into the "study house" of the deeper mysteries. The practitioner must embody the various dimensions of reality, separating the transcendent and the corporeal to rectify the confusion left by Adam and Eve.

The Flood

The world remains in the maelstrom of the flood. Flood traditions and motifs represent the dilemmas of contemporary society. The *Ra'aya Meheimna* and *Tiqqunim* culled many images of antediluvian chaos from the Bible and the Talmud: the talmudic "sea of Torah,"[53] the sea trial of the biblical Jonah, and the mysteriously allegorical *aggadot* about Raba Bar Bar Hanah.[54]

The flood's chaos is a plague of decrees of the harshest, most immediate judgment, which are like the turbulent sea.[55] The spiritual elect, besieged by the forces of corruption take refuge in the ark. The recession of the flood indicates the beginning of a messianic age. The ark is the Zohar,[56] which provides its beleaguered community with shelter and salvific knowledge in the midst of the present chaos.[57]

The raven and the dove of the flood account have particular importance in *Tiqqueni ha-Zohar* and *Ra'aya Meheimna.* In the original account, of course, the raven perishes in the sea, whereas the dove returns to the ark to signal the eventual passage of the elect to safety. Two movements of Judaism are described, one of which failed in its mission, pulled down by the corrupting needs of an ignorant populace. The failure of the raven, the corrupted rabbinate, leaves the "dove" to reveal the redemptive process.

The *yonah,* or dove, represents the *Shekhinah,* who, like the dove, seeks a resting place, with Jerusalem as her nest.[58] The word *yonah* signifies both the willful prophet Jonah and the dove that is the agent of humanity's redemption.[59] The dove is the trustworthy messenger who archetypally guards her brood with prayers, songs, and praises.[60] The dove also represents Moses, who brings the Torah through which Israel is redeemed.[61] The political dilemma of Israel is portrayed as that of a dove being pursued by an eagle.[62]

As Yiẓḥak Baer has demonstrated, the parable of the dove bears remarkable similarity to a commentary on Jeremiah that originated among followers of the Abbot Joachim of Fiore. The Christian text is pseudepigraphic and apparently dates to 1240 C.E. It compares the ark with the besieged ecclesiastic community. The raven represents the dominant sect, whose fate is to be swallowed up by the crisis, whereas the dove represents the Joachide-Franciscans who will emerge to signal the coming redemption. This commentary also portrays a pantheon of nemeses: Dominican Catholicism, Greek Orthodoxy, the Roman clergy, rationalistic philosophers, and various other corrupting influences.

The possibility of contact between the mystical representatives of two largely antipathetic religious communities is perplexing. Baer was of the opinion that these pietists had been brought into "ideological kinship."[63] Baer theorized that the author of the *Tiqqunim* developed an interpretation of the dove, then came in contact with the Joachide account of the raven and incorporated it into his work. In Baer's words:

> Authors of sermons such as those of the *Ra'aya Meheimna* and the *Tiqqunei ha-Zohar* seem like the Jewish brothers of the wandering mendicant brothers, the spiritualized Joachide Franciscans from whom originated the anonymous commentary on Jeremiah. . . . There is no doubt that the Jewish Kabbalist heard or read the [pseudo-Joachim's] words and wanted to make use of them for his purposes, but he did not succeed in this, or perhaps he was not so brazen as to explain his allusions and left them unclear. He was certainly not so brazen as to apply the Messianic term "Yonah" to one of his own generation.[64]

Yiẓḥak Baer's studies of the *Ra'aya Meheimna* were directed towards tracing the interaction of the author with Christian pietistic circles in Castile. Evidence such as the parable of the dove and the raven, along with his advocacy of asceticism and self-abnegation pointed, in Baer's view, to a direct link between the two mystical communities. The methodological flaw in such a directed study was the narrow focus of the subject matter. Although there are similarities between these teachings and those of the author's Christian contemporaries, these teaching are not the main preoccupation of the *Tiqqunim* and *Ra'aya Meheimna*. The Zohar literature may borrow literary motifs from many sources, including Christian mystical texts, yet its attitude toward Christianity is savagely negative. In his eagerness to identify links between the author of *Ra'aya Meheimna* and his Christian contemporaries, Baer gave scant attention to the fact that their shared notions reflect the common values of pious ascetics in every culture.

Isaiah Tishby theorized that the raven represents a veiled critique of Moses de Leon, who was said to have profitted financially from the philanthropists who financed the "transcription" of the Zohar.[65] The reverence that the author directs toward the Zohar as a sacred text, however, would seem to belie such a sentiment. If the Zohar was really produced by a wider circle of initiates, then perhaps author of the *Tiqqunim* could revere the work as a whole while expressing disappointment in its principle contributor. The allusions to Moses' fall seem, most likely, to reflect the stormy interaction of mystical and halakhic communities.

The drama of the Day of Atonement is also symbolized by the events of the flood. In this metaphoric scheme, the flood signifies the events of the coming year and repentance is the soteric agency, saving the adherent from annihilation.[66] The predominance of this literary motif caused *Tiqqunei ha-Zohar* to be identified liturgically with the season of penitence from the month of *Elul* through the Day of Atonement. Many editions are divided in such a way as to guide the pious reader through a recitation of the whole *Tiqqunei ha-Zohar* during that forty-day period.[67] Clearly, the flood was popularly perceived as an important and characteristic motif in the *Tiqqunim*.

These interpretations present the flood as a recurring myth of renewal. The symbols and metaphors of the story provide a rationale for the social upheavals and arbitrary tragedies of the author's time.

The Incarnate Demonic

The historical catastrophes that attended the creation, the flood, and the exodus continue in the machinations of demonic. The author of the Zohar and the author of the *Tiqqunim* shared a very great dread of this *incarnate* demonic spirit. Such a notion of an independent realm of evil is close to dualistic heresy, a violation of classical Jewish theism. As such, these kabbalistic traditions balance various contradictory understandings of the demonic.

As has been stated, kabbalistic thought wavered between the poles of Neoplatonic optimism and gnostic pessimism.[68] The former is a monistic understanding of a world nourished and sustained by the outpourings of Divine effluence. The latter posits a barrier between the mystic, mired in the banality and pain of present reality, and the sublime Divinity, in its own abode, forever elsewhere. A gnostic rupture in the Divine effluence may come about through the blocking effect of the *qelippot*. This catastrope creates a voided, demonic context. Similarly, in the Neoplatonic understanding, linear distance between the acme of the Godhead and the lowest hypostasis of the *sefirot* creates an alienation that provides a context for evil.[69] Both doctrines of evil exist *in potencia,* and both possibilities were incorporated into early kabbalistic systems.

The Zohar contains two understandings[70] of the origin of the demonic. One is a mythological, cathartic view of evil as Divine waste, and the other is a philosophical, emanative view, positing evil as part of linear distance from the acme of the Godhead. Both hold that evil emanates from the demonic that has its root in the left side of the Divine. Such understandings of evil preoccupied the early kabbalists of Provence and Gerona.[71] This view is reflected in the views of the Castilian practitioners of "gnostic Kabbalah," the brothers Jacob and Isaac Cohen and Todros Abulafia (himself an important influence on Moshe de Leon). The Cohen brothers seem to have been influenced by the Catharite gnostics of Languedoc, through the intermediary of the Provencal kabbalists.[72] In R. Isaac Cohen's scheme, the demonic originated in the *sefirah Binah,* the principle of Divine understanding in the upper triad of the sefirotic tree. R. Moses de Burgos posited evil as coming from the *sefirah* of *Gevurah* or Divine Judgment, which emanates out of *Binah.* In each situation, the kabbalist's see evil as nascent in the Divine structure. In the Zohar's emanative scheme, the demonic realm is commonly portrayed as a mirror image of the Divine sefirotic tree, though its power and scope are but a "dry shadow" of the holy emanation, "like a monkey to a person."[73] These mirror images of the sefirotic structure derive from the realm of *tum'ah* (impurity) and are called, variously, the "crowns of sorcery" or the "ten weapons of sorcery and witchcraft."[74]

The Zohar's second understanding portrays evil as originating in the residue of *Din,* which is produced in the same way that the human body produces impurity and waste.[75] Symbolically, these forces of evil and impurity also originate in the dregs of the primordial chaos, *tohu va-vohu.*[76]

The demonic may be incarnate in various ways. In its incarnation as the *yeẓer ha-ra',* or evil urge, it embodies the act of seduction. In its personification as the *Satan,* or accuser, it is the power of prosecution (*qitrug*) made manifest. In the persons of the *mashḥit* (destroyer) and the Angel of Death, it embodies destruction and death. In the persona of the horned Samael and his mates, it governs the demonic and personifies sexual transgression. There are evil spirits that take charge of various times and periods,[77] and demonic entities that command independent conceptual realms, such as that of falsehood.[78] The processes of the demonic, particularly in its incarnation as the evil inclination, are "as inexorable as leaven in dough."[79]

The demonic is also manifested in specifically masculine and feminine aspects. This male aspect is called *king of the gentiles*[80] and presides over a court of minor demons who serve him.[81] Lilit, the archetypal devouring goddess of crib death and nocturnal emission, is a palpable presence in *Tiqqunei ha-Zohar*'s demonology.[82] She is the incarnate product of incest and miscegenation, *'ervat ishshah u-vitah,*[83] the "shadow" of the *Shekhinah,* who governs the realms of sin and despair.[84] In sefirotic terms, Samael and Lilit are justaposed to the *sefirot Tif'eret* and *Malkhut.*

The author of the *Tiqqunim* is concerned mainly with the incarnation of the demonic in the world of the adept. He presents a demonological roster with angelic, anthropomorphic demons, and even "Jewish demons," who piously submit to the will of God: "There are three species of them: One species is like ministering angels, another is like human beings, another is like animals; some are wise in the Written and Oral Torah. . . . Ashmedai is their king, with all his family, for haven't we learned of the 'Jewish demons,' who submit to the Torah and the names of the Torah."[85]

Evil is personified in the *yeẓer ha-ra'*, or "evil inclination." The view of traditional Judaism identifies this force with the individual's inner propensity for evil. The author describes the *yeẓer ha-ra'* as empirical and independent, a "Jewish demon" (*shed yehudi*),[86] ruling over the wicked.[87] In submitting to it, one loses oneself to idolatry[88] and death.[89] This shadow is present in anger, pursuing the individual through his emotional weaknesses: "The Blessed Holy One orders bringing gifts to the priest, whose blessings of mercy overcome the anger that is incited in one through the gall, the sword of the angel of death . . . "[90]

The internal struggle against the *yeẓer ha-ra'* is really a struggle against an outside force, Samael.[91] The soul is a battlefield that the holy and the demonic fight to control: "*And a man struggled with him* (Genesis 32:26) for his *miẓvot* and sins were struggling to do battle from the realm of *miẓvot*; *And he saw that he could not overcome him,* from the realm of the sins . . . "[92]

The struggle is unending; for the power of evil corresponds to the adept's own spiritual possibilities: "One has a *yeẓer ha-ra'* along the lines of a lion, like a donkey, like a serpent, one's *yeẓer ha-ra'* goes with your character and the potentials of hour . . ." [93]

This struggle, in the practitioner's personal myth, is an essential fact of existence for "if the Blessed Holy One hadn't created the *yeẓer ha-tov* and the *yeẓer ha-ra',* which are light and darkness, there would have been no sin and *miẓvah* for the man of *Beriah.*"[94] The heroism required for the struggle against the evil inclination comes from the *sefirah Gevurah,* the quality necessary for the battle against passion.[95] The weapon in this struggle is the adept's Torah study, after the rabbinic dictum: "If the *yeẓer ha-ra'* attacks you, take it to the House of Study."[96]

The Demonic in the Social Order

In addition to the adept's inner struggle, the author understood the demonic as manifesting itself most openly in the social order. Demonic elements include the *'ammei ha-areẓ,* "people of the land" or ignoramuses, and the *'erev rav* or "mixed multitude" of the Exodus account.

The *'erev rav* are at least partially responsible for society's degeneracy. These progeny of Lilit [97] are *inherently* flawed or inferior members of the Jewish community. According to the metaphor of the *Tiqqunim,* the *'erev rav* have the worth, to society, of fertilizer decaying in a garden: "This is the realm of the mixed multitude: garbage is mixed in the garden, to grow seeds from the realm of the Tree of Knowledge of Good and Evil, from the realm of idolatry that is called Saturn, Lilit. It is rotting garbage, because of the excrement mixed with all kinds of filth and reptiles with dead dogs and asses thrown upon it . . .[98]

Besides being agents of decay, the mixed multitude generate ritual impurity, a halakhic status that Kabbalah fetishized as actively demonic. Not only are the pious condemned to exile, but the *'erev rav,* who are under the command of Satan,[99] are banished among them:[100] "Lilit is the Mother of the *'erev rav,* who pollutes through sitting like a menstruous woman. So also, the *'erev rav* defile wherever they sit, as a menstruous person would, for any of the righteous who must sit among them."[101]

The great fallen biblical races, the *Amaleqim, nefilim, gibborim, refaim,* and *anaqim,* make up yet another demonic caste in contemporary human history.[102] They are also incarnate in the arrogant generation of the Tower of Babel, ignorant, brazen, and philanthropically inconsistent. These five races, primordial enemies of Israel, are Judaism's contemporary nemeses. To the pietistic author, each of these five groups represents one aspect of social malaise. This typology further demonstrates his alienation from the communal leadership and authority.[103]

Amaleqim, "Amalekites," are distinguished by their lawlessness. They corrupt the young and the spiritually weak, just as the biblical Amaleq attacked the younger and weaker Israelites. *Nefilim,* the fallen angels (cf. Genesis 6:4), have allowed philosophy and heresies to corrupt their belief and thus fell from their spiritual plane. *Gibborim,* the biblical "men of renown" are characterized by their social self-aggrandizement. In Yiẓḥak Baer's opinion, these are the court Jews with their intrigues. *Refaim,* in a play on the Hebrew *rofef,* "soften," are those who "soften" their religious observance to assimilate.[104] The *anaqim,* "giants," are the wealthy, who are miserly with their support of the mendicant scholars.[105] A subtext in the presentation of these typologies is Kabbalah's ongoing polemic against the corrosive influence of philosophical rationalism on the observance of the commandments.

The *bor* or "ignoramus" is another agent of the demonic. This is understood as a multivalenced term, meaning either "pit" or, roughly, "boor." *Tiqqunei ha-Zohar* explores this multivalence, quoting the talmudic dictum *Ein bor yere ḥet* (the *bor* cannot be in fear of sin).[106] *Bor* signifies, as well, the pit into which Joseph was thrown by his brothers.[107] According to a well-known midrash,[108] the pit was full of snakes and scorpions, which are interpreted as "famine, thirst, weeping, fasting, and darkness."[109]

One's social caste is intrinsic, deriving from the state of the practitioner's soul:

> There is a soul that is like a slave, as it says: *When a man sells his daughter as a slave* (Exodus 21:7). There is a soul that is like a common maidservant, even as there are people who are slaves, and sometimes the soul reincarnates, as it says: *The dove could find no rest for the sole of her foot* (Genesis 8:9), and the evil inclination chases after it to enclose it in a body, which is the maidservant of the evil inclination, which is a Jewish demon![110]

The author of the *Tiqqunim* polemicizes against various community members and agitate for the moral betterment of the community or individuals. Yet, because the state of the individual's soul is intrinsic, this polemic can improve their behavior to only a certain degree. The possibilities of flawed souls remain limited:

> The Masters of the Mishnah taught that there are those who are like ministering angels. These are the sages who know what has been and what will be, and in their image on the earth are the masters of philosophy, the astrologers of Israel who know what has been and what will be from the signs of the waning of the sun and the moon, every star and constellation and what the world shows them. And there are those who rut like animals; the Masters of the Mishnah taught that they are like reptiles, their daughters are like vermin, of whom it says: *Cursed be he who lies with any beast* (Deuteronomy 27:21). They hate the sages, the Masters of the Mishnah, who are truly like the ministering angels. Thus the Masters of the Mishnah taught one only seek guidance from one who is like an angel of the Lord of Hosts. And there are others, Masters of the Secrets of the Torah, Masters of qualities who inherit their souls from the realm of the holy monarchy that is made up of the ten *sefirot*. For whoever inherits this and is worthy of it is worthy of the undivided ten *sefirot*.[111]

Hence the spiritual state of the various community members of the Jewish community ultimately rests on the condition of their souls. Such a condition can be improved only through exposure to the secrets of the Kabbalah through the efforts of the *maskil*.

The enmity between the learned and the *'ammei ha-areẓ* dates from the revelation at Sinai.[112] Nonetheless there is the possibility of a positive model of religious naiveté in the figure of the "good" *'am ha-areẓ*.[113] It is not surprising that, having maligned the scholars of the day so roundly, this mystic would present a model of naive, popular piety.

The triumph of the demonic is Israel's exile and subjugation by the nations of the world. This situation is mediated by the angels and demons, who administer the fate of Israel and the gentiles. The *Tiqqunim* are more conciliatory towards Islam than toward Christianity,[114] whose very nature is demonic. References to *Edom* and *Esau* refer to the Christian world,[115] whereas Islam is symbolized by *Miẓraim*, Egypt. Traces of anti-Christian polemic surface in dialogues between patricians and Jews based on rabbinic models.[116]

The world of chaos certainly awaits the redemption at the end of history. The Messiah who haunts the *Tiqqunim* and *Ra'aya Meheimna* is suffering and destitute, pursued by predators and abused by the rich. His nature is aptly portrayed by the suffering servant of the fifty-third chapter of Isaiah, languishing, imprisoned by the forces of evil.[117] This suffering Messiah is distinct from the heroic Davidic paradigm. Each of the traditional images of the Messiah is necessary, as the two Messiahs represent two sefirotic aspects of the redemption: "In the last redemption, [God] will send two Messiahs with you, according to the two wings of the dove, for in the fourth redemption you will be like a torso without limbs. Initially Israel was like a torso, and you [Moses] and Aaron were like the two dove's wings, with which Israel flew."[118]

In *Ra'aya Meheimna* and *Tiqqunim*, messianic associations are attached to the figure of Moses, the "once and future" leader, more than to any other figure.[119] The talmudic tradition of the forty-nine gates of awareness[120] that were given to Moses is interpreted in sefirotic terms. The seven lower *sefirot* each contain, potentially, seven further *sefirot*, leading to the charged figure forty-nine that indicates the level of Moses' consciousness. The Messianic age will bring a renewed Torah from Moses, encompassing the union of the lower and the intermediate *sefirot*:

> At the end of Moses' life in the last generation, he will reveal *Only that shall happen which has happened* (Ecclesiastes 1:9). . . . There is no generation less than 600,000, of which it says the *promise He gave for a thousand generations* (Psalms 105:8) and he [Moses] extended through every generation, in every saint and sage that preoccupies himself with Torah, up to 600,000, to correct the blemish of each one. And the meaning of the term is *He was wounded because of our sins* (Isaiah 53:5) that he is weighed against all of them, as the Masters of the Mishnah said[121] that one woman bore 600,000, implying Moses who is like 600,000.[122]

Moses is the valiant enemy of the realm of *qelippah*.[123] When he is overcome by catastrophes of misjudgment, his punishment is death and burial "in the Mishnah," entombment in the mundanity of the exoteric tradition.[124] As will be demonstrated in the fifth chapter of this study, Moses' fall is interpreted as an entanglement in the purely legalistic and casuistic dimension of the law. This flawed understanding is seen as a kind of violence against the Torah, as opposed to the Zohar's form of mystical speculation.

The State of the Shekhinah

The qualities of brokenness and disorder that characterize the nature of present existence are inherent in the *sefirah Malkhut.* This *sefirah* is the context into which the Divine effluence of the other *sefirot* flows. Because it is the beginning of existence, the base of the sefirotic tree, *Malkhut* is where humanity encounters the Divine. As is widely known, *Malkhut* is most often evoked in the figure of the *Shekhinah,* the symbolization of the Divine feminine.

The symbolic imagery for the *Shekhinah* is the richest of all the theosophic Kabbalah. This process of symbolization is quite evident in the *Bahir,*[125] the earliest work of theosophical Kabbalah. The *Bahir* personified the *Shekhinah* archetypally as bride,[126] princess, *ecclesia* of Israel, and simply *Shekhinah.* The *Bahir* also symbolizes the *Shekhinah* archetypally as earth, moon, citron, and date.

Tiqqunei ha-Zohar draws from the rich store of images for this *sefirah.* A number of characteristic symbolizations may demonstrate the author's preoccupations. In levirate marriage and annulment, she is the shoe of rejection, because she represents the banality of the physical dimension.[127] Elsewhere, the *Tiqqunim* portrays the *Shekhinah* as the *ur*-mother, mistress of the Divine house,[128] bound to Israel and bearing her vicissitudes,[129] the earthly incarnation of the Divine.[130] She has a special relationship with the sages, for "in exile, she rests on the Torah students like the Divine spirit that hovered over the watery chaos."[131] Positive images of the *Shekhinah* portray her as the *pardes* (garden) of the Torah, in that she encompasses the four exegetical levels of PaRDeS.[132]

Shekhinah embodies a number of dichotomous relationships. She encompasses both the negative potentials of the *sefirah Gevurah* on the left side of the sefirotic tree and the positive qualities from the *sefirah Ḥesed* on the right side.[133] The unification of both aspects takes place through the actions of the demiurgic figure of Metatron.[134] The condition of *Malkhut* is itself a mixture of good and evil;[135] its qualities of embodiment and incarnation are constantly shifting: "Like silver mixed with dross, she is a tree whose bark is unclean from without while its essence is sweet within . . . "[136] This dual nature is acknowledged in the prohibition of mixing wool and linen in one garment, which is a metaphysical expression of the dual nature nascent in *Malkhut*.

These themes of wholeness and partiality are evoked in the seven week transition from the Passover to the Shavuot festival. The Passover table's broken *maẓẓah* represents the demonic realm of the left, while the whole *maẓẓot* that envelope it derive their sacredness from the redemptive, inclusive realm of *Tif'eret*.[137] In kabbalistic terms, the *leḥem 'oni*, "bread of poverty," represents the union of the *sefirah Yesod,* the nexus of sexuality, and *Malkhut*. In this way, wasting bread is compared to the taboo of masturbation, which is, after all, "wasting seed."[138] These images of incompleteness and completeness are mirrored liturgically in the recitation of the complete *Hallel* prayers on the first day of the festival, followed by the incomplete *Hallel* on the subsequent days.[139] In this way, the mystical experience of Passover invokes the pathos of the *Shekhinah* in her exile, at the outset of the redemption. The ensuing forty-nine days are a meditation on the repair of the seven intermediate *sefirot* to unify them by the festival of Shavuot, which commemorates the theophany at Sinai.

The Immanence of God in *Tiqqunei ha-Zohar*

The chaos that is rife in the created world is mitigated, to some extent, by the immanent presence of God. Isaiah Tishby and Gershom Scholem[140] have portrayed a doctrine of Divine immanence specific to the *Ra'aya Meheimna* and the *Tiqqunim. Tiqqunei ha-Zohar* and *Ra'aya Meheimna* employ the doctrine of the four worlds of creation, *Aẓilut, Beriah, Yeẓirah* and *'Asiyyah*. According to Gershom Scholem,[141] the doctrine of the four worlds may have derived from contemporary gnostic ideas. It also owes much to early Kabbalah's adoption of the Neoplatonic concept of hypostases, progressive emanations of Divine effluence.

The Zohar hardly explores the juxtaposition of the terms *Bara-Yaẓar-'Asah.*[142] It describes the *sefirot* as extensions of God, linear hierarchies of Neoplatonic, hypostatic emanation. The higher *sefirot* are necessarily closer to the essence of the Godhead, whereas the lower *sefirot* are that much more alienated from this pure essence. The undifferentiated, abstracted Divine is called *Aẓilut,* or emanation. This undifferentiated realm is also called the *'alma de-yiḥudah,* or "world of unity," as opposed to the *'alma de-perudah,* or "differentiated world." The ultimate abstraction is also called *Ein Sof,* "infinity," or *Ayin,* the "nothingness" that stands at the peak of the Godhead.[143]

Tiqqunei ha-Zohar and *Ra'aya Meheimna* use of this idea, showing the influence of the *Masekhet Aẓilut,* an early fourteenth-century work, as well as the writings of R. Isaac of Acre. Scholem noted, in the *Tiqqunim,* three applications of the doctrine of the four worlds.[144] The first consists of the worlds as denoted without their formal names.[145] The second usage involves the terms *sefirot of Aẓilut, sefirot of Beriah* and so forth.[146] Finally the worlds are expressed anthropomorphically the structures "Adam of *Aẓilut,* Adam of *Beriah."*[147] For example,[148]

> Primordial Man [*Adam Qadma'ah*] [is] from the realm of purity, for there is another *Adam,* from the realm of impurity, and what's more, there are three "Adam's": Primordial *Adam,* who is the *Adam* of *Beriah, Adam* of *Yeẓirah, Adam* of *'Asiyyah* from the realm of purity. And there is another from the realm of impurity, the worthless *Adam* (*Adam Beliyya'al*), a man of sin, the Evil Inclination. The good *Adam* is the Good Inclination, as the elders have said (Ecclesiastes 7:14) *The one no less than the other was God's doing . . .*

The anthropomorphic employment of the doctrine of the worlds also posits a separate realm of the demonic. This *Adam Beliyya'al* is apparently a shadow of the Adam of *'Asiyyah,* the lowest world. Otherwise, there does not seem to be an independent realm of the demonic associated with this doctrine, only a duality at the level of *'Asiyyah* much like the phenomenon of the demonic at the *sefirah Malkhut*.

Tiqqunei ha-Zohar and *Ra'aya Meheimna* understand the *sefirot* as *vessels* for the essence of God. These vessels are distinct, but not entirely separate, from the undifferentiated unity of *Aẓilut*.[149] In these later compositions, the emanation of the Divine takes place across three realms: *Ein Sof*, the infinite abstraction of God; *'aẓmut*, the essence of God; and *kelim*, the vessels.[150] The *sefirot* are powers or qualities of God, but they have no existence in and of themselves.[151] They are called *temunat ha-Shem*, the "image of the Divine," the medium through which the immanent Divine reigns equally in all dimensions of existence.

According to this doctrine of immanence, *'Illat ha-'Illot*, the "Cause of Causes," the most transcendent aspect of God, extends through the medium of the *sefirot* into corporeality.[152] One common paradigm of this immanent emanation is the linear understanding of the emanation through the name *YHVH*.[153] In this paradigm, each letter of the Divine name represents one or more *sefirot*, so that every recitation of the name in prayer is a meditation on the sefirotic structure of the the universe. All the names and *kinnuyim* of God are signs, pointing to the *sefirot*, which in turn point to the Divine.[154]

'Illat ha-'Illot is distinguished by its dynamic qualities. In the *Ra'aya Meheimna* and *Tiqqunim*, *Ein Sof*, "Infinity," is identified with *'Illat ha-'Illot* and also with *Keter*, the uppermost *sefirah*.[155] At these levels of *Aẓilut*, there is unity of the essence and the *sefirot*: "One doesn't say of *'Illat ha-'Illot*, 'He said to *Keter*, let us make man . . . ,' He said to them 'Let your ears hear what your mouth says . . . '"[156]

This allusive remark indicates that the doctrine of God's immanence preserves the personal God of the Bible from the Zohar's monistic tendencies. The theological applications of this doctrine of immanence bring kabbalistic theology from the detached, monistic stance of the Zohar into a "theistic, personalistic"[157] understanding of God, creator and first cause, whose existence transcends all corporeality and is distinct from the Divine essence. The mechanistic formulations of the Zohar and the abstractions of Maimonidean theory were reformulated in a manner more theologically consistent with classical prophetic understandings of God's relationship to humankind.

In the *Tiqqunim*, God retains a quality of extreme hiddenness but is also present in the corporeal world. Hence, even the most divided and fallen aspects of the *Shekhinah*'s realm of *Malkhut* are redeemed by God's immanent nature. The Divine is available to illuminate the adept or the simple pietist with the personalism of the biblical God, who may be approached by anyone but particularly by His elect. Like Noah, the Patriarchs, and Moses, the *maskilim* are enfranchised to approach God and petition for the redemption of the people. Thus, the cataclysmic events of Genesis continue to unfold in the author's unified myth of present chaos.

5

Halakhah and Kabbalah

Tiqqunei ha-Zohar and *Ra'aya Meheimna* portray the *maskil's* relationship with agents of the exoteric Torah, the rabbis who apply legal authority, in complex and ambivalent terms. This relationship is generally interpreted as comprising a critique of *halakhah,* the legal dimension of rabbinical Judaism. The substance of this critique was utilized in the theoretical literature of the Sabbatean and Ḥasidic movements.

The conflict between the halakhic and kabbalistic traditions originates in the distinctions between the Torah's mystical nature and its exoteric character. In most cases, the practitioner was forced to choose between a mystical consciousness and a legalistic consciousness.[1] The *Tiqqunim* and *Ra'aya Meheimna* conduct a polemic, advocating the former over the latter.

The Two Torahs

The *Tiqqunim* and *Ra'aya Meheimna* portray two aspects of the Torah: the Torah of *Aẓilut* (emanation) and the Torah of *Beriah* (creation). The doctrine of the two Torahs is a mythic expression of the distinction between the Torah's exoteric and the esoteric levels. The author of these works derived this idea from certain dualistic images in the Bible.

In mythic terms, these two kinds of Torah were conceived separately, in the aftermath of the fall. They originate in the two World Trees in the garden of Eden. The *Eẓ Ḥayyim,* or Tree of Life, is synonymous with the Torah of *Aẓilut,* whereas the *Eẓ ha-Da'at Tov ve-Ra',* or Tree of Knowledge, is identified with the Torah of *Beriah.* The model practitioner is the *ẓaddik* (saint) of the Tree of Knowledge, rather than the mere "man" of the Tree of Life.[2]

Moses' breaking the first tablets of the Torah, in the incident of the golden calf, was another catastrophe that exacerbated the division between these two aspects of the Torah.[3] The first tablets represented the spiritual essence of the Torah, the Torah of *Aẓilut,* which is now available only to mystics. The second tablets constitute the Torah of *Beriah,* which is characterized by historicity. Its commandments are the product of this Torah's shell or *qelippah.* Hence, preoccupation with the mere commandments is an embrace of the most extraneous, irrelevant aspect of the Torah.

The two Torahs' functions are also understood in sefirotic terms, as stages in the path of the emanation of Divine effluence. The Torah of *Aẓilut* comprises the energies of the *sefirah Ḥokhmah* that are gathered under the *sefirah Tif'eret.* This is the undifferentiated Torah whose origins precede the creation of the world.[4] In one example from the *Tiqqunim,* the *maskil's* relationship with the Tree of Life, and its accompanying Torah of *Aẓilut,* is depicted in terms of a halakhic metaphor:

> The Masters of the Mishnah taught:[5] *One doesn't climb a tree or straddle it or use it.* I ask you, O Holy Spark, not in the simple, physical manner of the Masters of the Mishnah, but in the secret way, the spiritual way, as it says: *The maskilim will shine.* He said to him: "O venerable sage,[6] I will tell you, for you are from the realm of the Tree of Life, which is planted in the Sabbath Queen, which needs no person to tend it, as has been learned:[7] *He who uses the crown will depart.*[8]

The speaker asks Shimon Bar Yoḥai to explain the law in which trees may be part of a Sabbath boundary. The law is a metaphor for the way that the Tree of Life is defiled by the prosaic legalism of the Torah of *Beriah.* Using the Tree is like violating the *eruv,* the Sabbath boundary portrayed metaphorically as the boundary between the sacred and the profane.

The Torah of *Beriah* relates to the realm of the *Shekhinah,* the realm of the differentiated world.[9] This Torah is the outer garment of the *Shekhinah,* its debased aspect.[10] There are dangers in mistaking the essence of the Torah for its garment. The perverse behavior of the rebelious son, as portrayed in the Passover liturgy is one example of this mistaken world-view:

> There is a Torah of *Beriah* and a *Ḥokhmah* of *Beriah* and a *Binah* of *Beriah* and so it is with all the qualities (*sefirot*). In this Torah the son may be without *miẓvah* and *miẓvah* separated from the Torah. Hence: the rebellious son. But from the realm of *Aẓilut* there is no separation. One is in no danger of sin; and there is no punishment and no reward and no death. This Torah is the Tree of Life, the reward of the world-to-come, for this Tree of Life is called the world-to-come. But for the rebellious son, it is not called reward because this son did not strive in the Torah to receive a reward, not in action, speech, or thought. [11]

The rebellious son is a metaphor for the practitioner of the exoteric Torah, the legalist or rationalist who sees no deeper meaning to the commandments than their exoteric nature.

There is an internal contradiction in the doctrine of the two aspects of the Torah. The exoteric levels of rabbinic scholarship, preoccupation with the biblical text and the law, are also essential aspects of the Divine, not misapprehensions of it. Yet they remain a covering for the primordial, inner Torah. *Halakhah* determines the adept's corporeal existence, but kabbalistic wisdom is understood as the vessel for the channeling of Divine effluence, the stuff of enlightenment.[12]

The potentially antinomian possibilities of this doctrine engrossed the Jerusalem scholars of Jewish historiography: Yiẓḥak Baer, Gershom Scholem, and the latter's disciple, Isaiah Tishby. These scholars were influenced by the subsequent application of these ideas, particularly their eschatological aspect, in the Sabbatean heresy.

Gershom Scholem defined the tensions regarding Torah and law in the *Tiqqunim* in terms of two questions: the relationship of the Torah to the fall of man, and the messianic Torah.[13] In Scholem's view, the author of the *Tiqqunim* recognized the legitimacy of rabbinic Judaism. He also, however, viewed rabbinic Judaism as a mediating garment, which would be removed in the messianic age. According to Scholem, the author considered the Oral Torah as the less legitimate version of reality. This understanding had a definite utopian-eschatologian application, which was to find expression in Sabbateanism.[14]

Yiẓḥak Baer understood the doctrine of the two Torahs as a revolt against the rabbis of the age, part of a pattern of uprisings against leadership of all the Western religions. All the same, he did not view it as a campaign against rabbinic Judaism. According to Baer, the author's ambivalence towards the *halakhah* derived from the tension between Jewish survival in the Diaspora and national yearnings. Out of this tension came a great yearning for the creation of a new Torah that would be wholly godly. Its practitioners would necessarily be pious ascetics primarily concerned with values of devotionalism, humility, and simplicity of thought.[15] This understanding is in keeping with Baer's general preoccupation with the eschatological and social aspects of the *Ra'aya Meheimna's* teachings, particularly as they resembled the writings and doctrines of his Christian contemporaries.

Isaiah Tishby has assembled the most exhaustive review, to date, of the various contradictory statements regarding the Torah in his master work, *Mishnat ha-Zohar.*[16] Tishby considers the author's distinctions and contradictions potentially irreconcilable: "[*Ra'aya Meheimna* and *Tiqqunim*] have a peculiar understanding of the role of the Torah. Rather than a harmony between the various aspects of the Torah, there is a confusion of divisions and chasms, with images of bitterness and ugliness. It is a Torah of changed intent, with images of exile and alienation predominating over enlightenment and spiritual purity. This area is also rife with internal contradictions."[17]

After an exhaustive analysis of many of the references to the exoteric tradition, Tishby concludes:

> I see no way of resolving such a multitude of inconsistencies. On the one hand, the author extols the *halakhah*, its literature, and those who teach and study it. On the other hand, he despises them as the straw and waste matter of the Torah, or as asses, and agents of the demonic. Any attempt to bridge the gap between these two diametrically opposed points of view is doomed to failure. . . . We find ourselves face to face with an extraordinary kabbalist who, for unknown reasons, perhaps connected with his own personal psychology or with some social situation, tried to have the best of both worlds, seeking both to glorify and destroy rabbinic tradition. . . . My view, in brief, is that the author of the *Ra'aya Meheimna* had antinomian tendencies, but was careful not to express himself entirely negatively, even with respect to the Messianic age.[18]

Perhaps a review of the author 's portrayal of the tension between Kabbalah and *halakhah* will further clarify his attitude toward the *halakhah* and its agents. Rather than examine every contradictory reference to the subject, I will examine themes that are recurrent or, in the case of contradictions, dominant.

The Mystic and the Law

The *Tiqqunim* and *Ra'aya Meheimna* seem to view rabbinic casuistry as unrelated to the principle aim of contemplative study, the redemption of the *Shekhinah,* the realm of present existence. The legal system of *halakhah* is often portayed as debased and temporary. This legal structure will, inevitably, be supplanted by the idealized and unrealized law that lies nascent in the secrets of Kabbalah.[19] Throughout the *Tiqqunim* and *Ra'aya Meheimna,* the author yearns for release from the rigid mentality of rabbinic casuistry.

In deprecating the exoteric level of the Torah, the author uses a number of midrashic and kabbalistic hermeneutical categories. One of these was the acronym *PaRDeS,* a term that was apparently originated by *Moshe de Leon. PaRDeS* distinguishes the levels of the exoteric and esoteric Torah in the following terms: *peshat* (simple meaning), *remez* (allegory), *derash* (midrash), and *sod* (the esoteric meaning).[20] Two changes in terminology are characteristic of the *Tiqqunim's* typology: the use of the term *re'ayot*[21] instead of *remez* and the denigratory *pi shoneh halakhot*[22] instead of *peshat.*[23] The strength of the *PaRDeS* formula is that it implies that the four levels of the Torah are coexistent with one another. This conciliatory position derived from classical rabbinic understandings of the Torah's multiplicity of meaning. The author of the *Tiqqunim,* however, utilized the typologies of *PaRDeS* to stress his pejorative view of the literal meaning of the text.

The four dimensions of the Divine text are also metaphors for the cosmic structure and the stages of mystical inquiry. The achievement of the Torah's fourth and deepest level, *sod,* is the goal of mystical quest. This is in keeping with another important theme in the *Tiqqunim,* that of transition from demonic triunity to redemptive quaternity. Elsewhere, however, these four aspects of the Torah are described as sustenance for the soul,[24] the *merkavah* or vehicle of enlightenment.[25]

Tiqqunei ha-Zohar and *Ra'aya Meheimna* employ the signifiers *peshat,* the simple meaning of the text, and *pesaq,* the determination of the law, to deprecate the significance of the exoteric Torah. In fact, the author interprets many technical expressions of the halakhic process as signifiers for aspects of existence in the realm of the *sefirah Malkhut.* In this way, the Masters of the Mishnah and the *posqei halakhot,* "determiners of the law," abuse the *Shekhinah* in her bitter exile.[26]

The questions, contradictions and lack of resolution that characterize the Talmud represent hidden and inchoate aspects of present existence. As such, they are instruments of survival in the benighted realm of *Malkhut:*

> With the addition of the letter *vav, pesaq* [literally, halakhic judgment] becomes *pasuq* [literally, verse]. The verse that contains all halakhic decisions, that are the *Shekhinah, tashbap,*[27] *shama'nu,*[28] *shitah,*[29] *tiyuvtah,*[30] *tosefta,*[31] *haggadah, tayqu*[32], *tania, Kabbalah, halakhah, mishnah, baraita, qushia,*[33] *maḥloqet, ḥumrah,*[34] and *qulah.*[35] The *Shekhinah* is in the question, which the sage asks relevantly and answers according to the *halakhah.*[36]

The confusion and randomness of the Talmud seem to derive from the absurdity of present existence. The author maligns that dimension of existence, the *halakhah* that governs it, and the rabbis who propagate *halakhah.* The realm of plain meaning is also described as demonic as a serpent's bite.[37] Even the cantillation point *sof pasuq,* "end of a verse," refers to *sof pesaq halakhot;* that is, "the end of law making!"[38] The Talmud itself is portrayed as a barrier, blocking the individual from the attainment of kabbalistic illumination. This relationship is even expressed in a halakhic metaphor: *halakhah* is like the stagnant water brought into the purifying pool, whereas Kabbalah derives from the pure rivers that nurture both the Garden of Eden and the Tree of Life.[39]

The Typologies of the Legalist and the Mystic

The author of the *Tiqqunim* objects to the halakhist's social role in a manner in keeping with his critique of the Jewish community.[40] Satirically, he refers to them as the *ḥamorei ha-Torah,* "donkeys of the Torah."[41] More lethally, they are also portrayed as venal opportunists, motivated by the desire for personal gain:

> Many masters of study, colleagues of yours, nightly cry out contradictions in the Oral Torah, crying like dogs who say "Hav hav!", as it is written (Proverbs 30:13) *The leech has two daughters, "Give" and "Give."*[42] Give us wealth in this world, give us wealth in the next world, as it is taught:[43] *Learn much Torah and you will be given much reward.* And there is no one who is occupied with the Torah in order to raise the *Shekhinah* from the Diaspora and to unite her with the husband, for their eyes are blind, and their hearts are sealed.[44]

The author of the *Tiqqunim* reordered the classical hierarchies of rabbinic authority. In a series of Hebrew puns, the talmudic scholars are portrayed as slaves in Egypt, embittering their own lives with the stringencies and refinements of the law: "The Masters of the Mishnah said: *They embittered their lives with hard work [avodah qashah]* (Exodus 1:14) with difficulties *with mortar [ḥomer]* with *kal va-ḥomerz*[45] with bricks [*levenim*] with tempering [*libbun*] of the *halakhah, with all the work in the field, that is baraita,*[46] *with all their work,* that is Mishnah."[47]

Elsewhere, this anonymous kabbalist employs plainly medieval imagery to illustrate the relationship between the halakhist and the mystic. The halakhists are portrayed as *ba'alei terisim,* "shield bearers," foot soldiers for the knights of the Kabbalah: "A voice calls out in the Academy: 'How many of you are shield bearers of the Oral Torah, come to do battle with the serpent?' "[48]

The actions of the shield bearers, however, are by definition futile: "The shield bearers come into the Academy; yet with their leniencies and stringencies, *They turn this way and that and there is no one* (Exodus 2:12)."[49]

The "shield" of the Oral Law is akin to the classical kabbalistic symbol of the *qelippah,* or shell, which separates the individual from the Divine.[50] Each is a barrier to deeper, more profound knowledge.

For the legalist and the mystic, coexistence is possible only if the legalist accepts a secondary role, creating the context for the mystic's erotic quest. *Tiqqunei ha-Zohar* and *Ra'aya Meheimna* employ two models to describe the positive function of the halakhists, the model of the foot soldier and the model of the stonecutter. In one text in particular, they play these roles almost simultaneously, storming the fortress of the *Matronita,* or *Shekhinah,* and building her a trysting place for union with the Godhead:

> There are men who exert themselves in the Oral Torah for its own sake; they are its artisans. There are those who cut stones, mountains and mighty rocks. Afterwards they perfect them with questions and of them it says: *Build it of whole stones* (Deuteronomy 27:6). With them they make many buildings for the King and Queen to dwell in. These decisions are garments for the Queen, they cut many facets into them, then perfect them with many questions, in which the *Matronita* may appear before the King. And at that time *you will see it as an everlasting covenant* (Genesis 9:16). These are the garments of the high priest, the four white garments and the four golden garments.[51]

At this point, the chisel of the stonecutter is transformed into the weapon of the foot soldier, as the halakhists become the infantry of the Divine army:

> These garments are the decisions of the shield bearers that come from the study house, who cut and set them with their tongues as with swords and lances, like horsemen on dry land and the sea, which are themselves the Written and the Oral Torahs. Happy are they, with the King between them, the central pillar, that encompasses the Written and Oral Torahs, which are given from the right and the left, with which they make war. Woe to those who go to battle without the King, of them it is written (Psalms 19:4): *There is no utterance, there are no words, whose sound goes unheard.* All of the artisans are found in the inner[52] Oral Torah as it says: *All the honor of the princess is within* (Psalms 45:14).[53]

The midrashic image of the hammer on the rock, giving off sparks in every direction, is the classical expression of the Torah's multiplicity of meaning.[54] In a further exploration of the image of stonecutting as a metaphor for rabbinic casuistry, the creation of Oral Torah is compared to Moses' violent striking of the rock at *Merivah* (Numbers 24:21). This catastrophe amounts to the rape of the *Shekhinah:*

> Moses' rock, of which it says: *You will speak to the rock before their very eyes and it will yield its water* (Numbers 20:8)—this is a Divine voice, on which is contingent only speech and supplication. But the maidservant is another rock that is called *Mishnah,* the feminine, slave, servant. Of it it says: *A slave cannot be disciplined by words* (Proverbs 29:19); rather he strikes it and connects from it various decisions and collects them and they are called collected . . . with no flow of wisdom or *Kabbalah.* My rock is called the Princess, so it says: *You will speak to the rock before their very eyes and it will yield its water,* with words and persuasion, like a Princess. Since he forced her and struck her, death was decreed for him. For one who refuses the *Matronita* incurs the death sentence, all the more so one who forces the princess. So it was decreed that he should not enter the land of Israel, to be buried in a strange land.[55]

Moses' violent disobedience creates a flawed tradition. His offense bars him from the land of Israel in the same way that casuistry bars the adept from enlightenment. This flawed hermeneutic originates with Moses, the *Ra'aya Meheimna* himself:

> You are the one of whom it says: *And he struck the rock* . . . (Numbers 24:21). For the Blessed Holy One instructed you to speak to the rock, and you did not do so, for if you had done it through speech they would be studying the Torah with no doubt, with no question and dispute. Because it says of you: *And he struck the rock* and nothing came of it but single drops, so the Masters of the Mishnah are like those who strike the rock. Their tongues are like a hammer striking the rock, they decide many halakhic decisions, which accumulate drop by drop.[56]

The motif of Moses' striking the rock reinforces the comparison of scholasticism to stonemasonry. The debased and degenerate *halakhah* is "the burial place of Moses."[57] Elsewhere, the rabbinic tradition is portrayed as a mining expedition that ends in disaster for its participants:

> Many Masters of the Mishnah have descended to the depths of the *halakhah* and have found the date of the liberation. Yet they have descended there and they have not escaped. Even though their language is like a hammer splintering a rock, their hammer is too exhausted to penetrate that rock, and whoever has done so without permission has been bitten by the serpent. And there are others who penetrated it until they came to the bottom of the primordial abyss, from which they have not escaped. . . . The Messiah, son of David, has fallen there with the Messiah, son of Joseph![58]

The halakhists lack the wisdom to predict the date of the messianic age, and their attempts lead to disaster.[59] The motif of the stonecutter predominates over that of the foot soldier. Rather than drawing off the flowing waters of kabbalistic wisdom, the halakhist chips and smashes the opaque crust of the Torah in images that invoke both violence and futility. The rabbinic hermeneutic is an act of violence against the Torah's essence.

Pardes

The well-known Rabbinic statement about the four who entered the *Pardes,* or mystical orchard, was particularly important in kabbalistic hagiography. The account stresses the pitfalls of the mystic quest and the idealization of Rabbi Akiva, who "entered in peace and departed in peace," as the paradigm of the integration of Law and mysticism.[60] This seminal account is, oddly, largely unexplored in the main sections of the Zohar.[61] It is cited repeatedly in the *Tiqqunim*[62] and *Ra'aya Meheimna,*[63] where it is presented as an example of the risks of mystical ascent. The author readily equates the Pardes, as orchard, with the multi-tiered hermeneutical PaRDeS.[64]

In the Tiqqunim, the four adepts parallel the four heads of the river that flowed through Eden, another mythical orchard.[65] In a pun, the river *Pishon* is *pi shoneh halakhot,* the "mouth teaching *halakhot,*" the Oral Torah:

> *It then divides and becomes four branches* (Genesis 2:10). These are the four that entered the *Pardes,* one went to *Pishon,* which is *pi shoneh halakhot.* The second rose to the *Giḥon,* and there it is buried, of which it says: *Anything that crawls on his belly* (Leviticus 11:42).[66] The third rose to the *Ḥideqel,* sharp and light,[67] this is the light and sharp language of *derasha.* The fourth entered *Perat,* which is the brain, which flourished and multiplies.[68] Ben Zoma and Ben Azzai went up in the *qelippin* of the Torah and were harmed by them. R. Akiva went up in the mind. Of him it is said that he went up in peace and departed in peace.[69]

The *avnei shayish tahor,* the stones of pure marble that are the object of Rabbi Akiva's warning, are understood by the author though a recurring theme of scholasticism as stonemasonry. These stones are the second tablets of the Torah, the result of the disaster of the golden calf. The three victims of the ascent erred in equating the prosaic stones of marble with the life-giving waters of the mystic wisdom:

> When Moses brought the two tablets of the Torah down to Israel, they were unworthy of them, and they were smashed, causing the loss of the first and second Temples. . . . He brought them others from the realm of the Tree of Knowledge of Good and, Evil, from which is brought the Torah of forbidden and permitted, from the right, life and, from the left, death, so Rabbi Akiva said to his students, "When you come to the pure stones of marble do not say 'Water, water.'" For the other stones are life and death, the heart of the wise on the right and the heart of the fool on the left. Moreover, you will endanger yourselves, for those of the Tree of Knowledge are in separation, while the stones of pure marble are in unity, with no separation at all.[70]

The reference to the stones is deliberately obscure in the Talmud's rendering, making it an appropriate object of subsequent exegesis. *Tiqqunei ha-Zohar* continues of the image of the Torah as stone, to be crafted or mutilated according to the expertise or the ineptitude of the scholar-adept.

In sefirotic terms, the three hapless Rabbis ascended only to the realm of *qelippah,* while Rabbi Akiva entered in the realm of *moḥin,* the Divine mind. This qelippah that entangles the three victims is compared to the foreskin that covers the uncircumcized *membrum viril:* "The four who entered the *Pardes* are from the realm of the foreskin. Three ate from those *qelippot* and died, and the fourth ate the inner fruit and threw out the *qelippot* and lived, just as Rabbi Meir found a pomegranate, ate its inner part and threw out the husk."[71]

Rabbi Meir, although a contemporary of Rabbi Akiva, is not a figure in the original *Pardes* account. His "discarding the husk" was an analogy for his continued study with the apostate Elisha Ben Abuya.[72] Here it is adapted as metaphor for the mystic's relationship to the exoteric Torah. The adept discards the husk of the *halakhah* to extract the deeper, kabbalistic meaning of the text.[73] This image is also employed in a national metaphor: "The pomegranate: Ben Zoma sinned with it, while Rabbi Meir ate the kernel and threw out the husk. For the husk are the nations of the world and Israel is the intellect within. In the same way, the *Shekhinah* is the *Pardes* in the exile, with the intellect within. It is called the nut, as King Solomon said *I went down to the nut garden* (Song of Songs 6:11), and the *Shekhinah* is the hidden fruit."[74]

So it is that the exoteric dimension of the Torah is a barrier or shell for the esoteric dimension.[75] The hapless victims, enmeshed in the *qelippot, saw and died,*[76] so that the malevolence of the three exoteric dimensions destroyed the victims of the ascent.[77] The negotiation of the treacherous *qelippot* is not merely the goal of personal quest, but has resonance for the fate of the Jewish people.

The Masters of the Mishnah

The way that *Tiqqunei ha-Zohar* and *Ra'aya Meheimna* employ the term *Masters of the Mishnah* is particularly complex. On one hand, the expression *as the Masters of the Mishnah established* is used frequently to introduce a Rabbinic dictum, be it *halakhah* or *aggadah,* which is then interpreted kabbalistically.[78] Nonetheless, the Masters of the Mishnah are caught in a prosaic level of consciousness:

> Fish and locusts require no ritual slaughter, only gathering. So it is that the masters of the Academy do not require ritual slaughter, rather it says of them: *Breathing his last, he was gathered to his people* (Genesis 49:33). Just as fish must live in the sea, so the sages, the Masters of the Mishnah, must live in the Torah; if they are taken from it, they die immediately. The *Tannaim* of the Mishnah proliferate in it like the fish in the sea, yet if they are on dry land and are thrown into the sea, not knowing how to swim, they die. But Adam the master of Kabbalah, which is above, is above them all. It says of him: *He will rule the fish of the sea and the birds of the air* (Genesis 1:26), who are the Masters of the Mishnah . . . during their study, they have disagreements and question one another, each swallowing his colleague . . . [79]

This ambivalence toward the Masters of the Mishnah extends to their source text, the Mishnah itself. As a result of its inherent duality, Mishnah can be a positive or a negative entity, according to the worthiness of its interpreter. There is, despite the images presented thus far, a positive aspect of the halakhist's struggle with the law. Sometimes, the Oral Torah is not malevolent, merely secondary:

> *The maskilim* are the masters of the biblical text *will shine,* these are the Masters of the Mishnah, for these Masters of the Mishnah are the forty-nine facets of purity and the forty-nine facets of impurity. . . .[80] The Masters of the Mishnah are illuminated in these forty-nine facets. They are second to the *halakhah,* its maidservant, just as Mordechai the Jew was second to the King.[81] So Mishnah is second to the king; the Masters of the Mishnah are illuminated in it. *Like the shining of the firmament;* this is the *halakhah,* the tradition to Moses from Sinai. It has many ladies in waiting, the legal decisions, the *maidens without number* (Song of Songs 6:8).[82]

The position of the Masters of the Mishnah, bound to time and space, is contrasted with the cosmic role of the *maskilim.* Nonetheless, the Talmud remains a valid path of ascent to the level of the *maskilim:*

> And she rises above them all, as it says: *You went above them all* (Proverbs 31:29) and she is with them all, as it says, *The law is like the majority. And those who lead the many to righteousness will be stars forever,* as the stars cannot be counted. And these "maidservants" (*'alamot*) call them, rather, worlds (*'olamot*). For the Righteous are like stars, each one has a star of his own; so our ancestors taught that every *ẓaddik* inhabits a world of his own.[83]

Then, in a significant fusing of angelology and kabbalah, the Mishnah is identified with Metatron,[84] the demiurgic go-between. In sefirotic terms, Metatron embodies the union of the lower *sefirot* and *Malkhut*. Contemplation of the Oral Torah brings the adept to the union of the lowest *sefirot*. All of the euphemisms of youth and servitude that are used to invoke Metatron also describe the functions of the exoteric Torah:

> And whoever achieves one *halakhah* inherits one world. All the more so for one who achieves a tractate, or two, or sixty,

> of whom it says: *There are sixty queens* (Song of Songs 6:8). For every tractate has the *Matronita* within it. Happy is he who inherits her in this world. The *halakhah* is the maidservant of the *Matronita,* Kabbalah. Happy are they who strive for the *Shekhinah* who is over everything, through *halakhah,* to free her from exile of which it says: *For your sins your mother was sent* (Isaiah 50:1), to escort her to her husband, that he might embrace her, as in: *His right hand under my head . . .* (Song of Songs 2:6). In the exile Mishnah, which is Mettatron rules, and it is *Mishneh la-Melekh,* the second to the King. Mishnah is the seat of the *Matronita.* And this is: *The maidservant who displaces her mistress* (Proverbs 30:23). And on the day of Moses the maidservant doesn't rule, rather the *Matronita.* After Moses died, Joshua, the youth, inherited, so the maidservant rules.[85]

Elsewhere, rabbinic hermeneutics, as well as the keeping of the commandments and the act of prayer, are described as Metatron's *tallit* or cloak.[86] Metatron's dominion of the lower *sefirot* is portrayed in terms of familiar social typologies: "There are two types of people who Metatron controls: the Masters of the Mishnah. *On the fish in the sea,* these are the sages. *The birds of the air,* these are the ones who have merit. *And on the beasts,* [these are] the ignorant."[87]

What is the true place of the Mishnah in the cosmic order? Although authority and dispute are canonized in the six portions of the *Mishnah,*[88] it remains the *mishneh la-melekh,* "second in command."[89] All images of six: the six measures of barley[90] that Boaz gave to Ruth (Ruth 3:15), the six orders of the Mishnah, and the sixty tractates of the Talmud,[91] represent stations in the mystic's ascent through the six intermediate *sefirot.*[92] These six realms of the forbidden and the permitted mirror the distinction between the legal dimension of the Torah and Kabbalah.[93]

The Oral Torah is barren because of its mundanity and accessibility. Denigrating the esoteric meaning in favor of the exoteric understanding destroys the meaning of existence, withdrawing the nurturing flow of the transcendent, turning the world into an arid landscape:

> When it is dry, it is dry land, the children below cry out for union, crying Hear O Israel, yet there is no voice and no answer, as (Proverbs 1:28) *Then they shall call me but I will not answer.* Therefore, one who excises the Kabbalah and Wisdom from the Oral and Written Torah, and discourages others from studying it, saying, "There is nothing but the simple meaning of the Torah and Talmud," has diverted the flow of the river from the Garden [of Eden]. Woe to him, better that he should not have been created in the world and not learned that Written and Oral Torah! He is like one who returns the world to the primordial chaos, causing poverty and extending the exile![94]

The strictures of the law themselves are not the negative aspect of the Oral Torah. Rather, the the object of criticism is the trivializing, casuistic rabbinical mentality, which invests all its effort in the pursuit of legalism: "Whoever puts aside the secret meaning, the essence of the two Torahs, has returned the world to the primordial chaos. These are the ones who say "There is no Torah other than the simple meaning, there is no other secret meaning!" And these facets [*parẓufin*] are the fifty-three [tractates of the Talmud], of which it says a *locked garden*[95] *is my sister my bride* (Song of Songs 4:12).[96]

The limitations of rabbinic consciousness cause the desolation of the Oral Tradition. Implicit in this criticism is the assumption that an unfettered consciousness would release some of the bonds of the law.

The Dividedness of the *Shekhinah*

In purely kabbalistic terms, present existence is that which takes place at the bottom of the sefirotic tree, in the *sefirah* of *Malkhut,* the domain of the *Shekhinah.* The rituals and strictures of rabbinic Judaism, which make up exoteric practice, are foremost an act of interaction with this *sefirah.* The *Shekhinah* suffers in exile, and the burden of the law is part of her suffering. The pluralism and multifacetedness of the Oral Torah derive from its flawed nature. The pettiness and sophistry of legalistic casuistry were also caused by these divisions in the realm of the *Shekhinah.*

Another kabbalistic paradigm describes the transcendent Written Torah as deriving from the *sefirah Ḥesed,* the realm of loving kindness. The exoteric Oral Torah derives from *Din,* the quality of harsh judgment.[97] Nonetheless, this Torah, which actualizes the Bible in present reality, is the domain of the *Shekhinah.* In kabbalistic terms, it is also the realm of the Torah of *Beriah* and the Tree of Knowledge. The *miẓvot,* commandments, form the medium of religious experience in the realm of *Malkhut.* The six higher *sefirot* remain ineffable, as "the Blessed Holy One is closed in the secrets of Torah as much as He is known in *miẓvot,* which are *Shekhinah.*"[98]

The Talmud's accumulation of unresolved conflicts and disputations is an overt sign of the dividedness of the *Shekhinah* and the unredeemed state of the law. The Talmud's myriad disputations (*maḥloqot*) contain both valid and invalid questions.[99] Some of these disputations originate in the uncleanliness of the divided realm of *Malkhut.*[100] Others derive from God's separation of the upper and lower waters during the act of Creation. These latter disputations, such as those of the *Tannaim* Hillel and Shammai,[101] are "for the sake of heaven, [and] will ultimately be upheld."

The duality of the Oral Torah is portrayed mythologically in the positive and negative aspects of the feminine *Shekhinah,* whose shadow is the demonic Lilit.[102] This duality is also portrayed in misogynist images of feminine inconstancy and instability:

> the woman who has pure and impure blood, from the realm of the Mishnah, she is not (Adam's) spouse, his unification, for there is no unification until the mixed multitude will be erased from the world. Therefore Moses was buried outside of the Holy Land, and his grave is the Mishnah, and no man knows his burial place to this day, for it was a tradition to Moses and the King, and the queen is separate from her spouse, therefore (Proverbs 30:21–23): *The earth shudders at three things . . . a slave who becomes king;* this is that slave, and the slave girl is the Mishnah. *A scoundrel sated with food,* the mixed multitude . . . [103]

The negative feminine may also be incorporated as an inherent part of the halakhist's consciousness:

> The Blessed Holy One said: *It is not good that man should be alone, I will make him a help-meet* (Genesis 2:18), this is the Mishnah, wife of that youth,[104] the maid servant of the *Shekhinah.* If Israel are worthy, she is a help to them in exile, from the realm of permitted, pure and *kasher.* If not, she is against them[105] from the realm of impure, unfit and forbidden. Permitted, pure, and *kasher* are from the realm of the good inclination; unfit, impure, and forbidden are from the realm of the evil inclination. And the woman, who has pure blood and blood of impurity, from the realm of the Mishnah . . . [106]

The Oral Torah is often symbolized and personified by the figure of the maidservant,[107] attending and doing the bidding of the Queen, Kabbalah: "*Like the shining of the firmament* . . . this is *halakhah,* which is Kabbalah to Moses from Sinai. And there are maidservants, directives of the law (*halakhot pesuqot*), of which it says *and damsels without number* (Song of Songs 6:8)."[108]

Symbolically, the *halakhah* may be "pure blood" or "blood of impurity"; that is to say, the demonic.[109] In a metaphoric use of the canon, the farthest exile of the *Shekhinah* is evoked in the conditions of the rabbinic *baraita,* the Tannaitic extranea in the Talmud.[110] These teachings are refuse left over from the refinement of the law: "*Baraita* is the *Shekhinah* from the left, as it says: For *she was found in the field* (Deuteronomy 22:27) and *Mishnah* is from the realm of the right, in union with the realm of the central pillar. Why are *Mishnah* and *Baraita* from the realm of right and left? Because of the ass (*ḥamor*) and the suspect bull that are to the right and the left.[111]

The *Shekhinah* is presently shrouded in the black garments of mourning, which consist of the mundane dimension of the Law. The *ẓaddik* strips away this literal meaning and clothes her in the true nature of the Torah.[112] The *maskil* must clothe the nakedness of the *Matronita:*

> When the Temple was destroyed, we learn that the slaves tore their hair and the men of action were called in the name of the *Matronita,* of whom it says (Proverbs 31:29): *Many women have done well and you surpass them all.* But . . . there is a *ẓaddik* whose merits and actions illuminate the *Matronita* and strip

her of her dark clothing of simple understandings and adorn her with garments of the shining hues of the secrets of the Torah.[113]

Rabbinic casuistries have the positive theurgic effect of increasing the necessary *Din,* or powers of judgment, in the world, which may be used to fight the enemies of Israel.[114] The very limitations of the law provide structure and context, almost like a crutch for the crippled *Shekhinah: "That which you reap* (Ruth 2:9), as it says, *an extended passage may not be truncated.*[115] These are the decisions of the Torah: forbidden and permitted, unfit and fit, impure and pure. And some fences must be made for the Torah, lest there be a rupture or a separation in the *Shekhinah,* the Oral Law. . . ."[116]

Just as there is a positive aspect to the work of the Masters of the Mishnah, there is a heroic aspect to rabbinic legalism, with all its dichotomies and dualisms. These nonetheless bring release from the dilemmas of humanity:[117] "*It separated the two waters* . . . (Genesis 1:7) polluted waters, pure waters, this is permitted, this is forbidden, this is fit, this is unfit, this is impurity, this is purity. These are the six tractates that are given to distinguish between good and evil, which Adam confused, he and the subsequent generations."[118]

The commandment of preoccupation with the Oral Law, then, is a mandate to distinguish between the admixtures of the holy and the demonic: "*That it may separate between water and water*... (Genesis 1:6) [God] separated the waters of purity, the fit and the permitted from the waters of the forbidden, the impure and unfitness, the waters of the broken well, putrid and filthy."[119]

This critique of legalism is the doctrinal parallel of the Zohar's criticism of the plain reading of the Torah and the philosophical rationalism. Two halakhic structures are really being presented: a debased casuistic form, which is opposed by a primordial and beautific reality originating from an idealized Mishnah. Talmudic casuistry can turn to sophistry, an empty, worthless realm. There is a "Mishnah of Truth," transcending the dichotomies of permitted-forbidden, pure-impure, and sacred-profane. The adept must synthesize these two dimensions of the law.

Various halakhic dicta reflect this tension. For instance, the Tannaitic directive that one must act on the topic at hand and reply with the appropriate ruling (*shoel ka-'inyan u-meshiv ka-halakhah*) is interpreted, in *Tiqqunei ha-Zohar,* as maintaining an esoteric consciousness while discoursing on the exoteric level.[120] In the same way, two biblical precepts involving the Torah invoke its dual nature. They are *Hagita bo,* the responsibility of study and preoccupation, and the commandment that the king copy out a Torah scroll. That latter *miẓvah,* the act of reproducing a perfect text, requires the quality of being unblemished attained by Jacob, the paradigm of *Tif'eret,* free of detritus, "for if the scroll is flawed, then it is disqualified."[121] Often these typologies are presented in the context of halakhic understandings of the vicissitudes of marriage. Hence, the exoteric law is allegorized as a kind of libel of the virginity of the bride, the supernal law.[122]

The coexistence of the legalist and the mystic is symbolized in the dual traditions of *halakhah* to Moses from Sinai and *kabbalah* to Moses from Sinai.[123] The intrusion of *halakhah* is portrayed as a rupture in the erotic union of the *Shekhinah* with the transcendent aspects of the Divine:

> This is the way that she goes up to him. Two thighs that are the two pillars of truth, and when she rises to the embrace of his two arms she is called *kabbalah.* And when she kisses him on the mouth she is called the Oral Torah, and at that moment what leaves the mouth of the king is upheld by the faithful shepherd. *With him I speak mouth to mouth* (Numbers 12:8). When she rises to her feet in the last exile she is called *halakhah* to Moses from Sinai, for the King is called *kabbalah* to Moses from Sinai . . . and when the *halakhah* becomes far from Moses, below, the *Shekhinah* becomes an argument with God. When she is not in his arms, *kabbalah,* there is a dispute above, hence: *Hear O Mountains the dispute of God* (Micah 6:2). These are the three Patriarchs, and their argument is the *Shekhinah,* for when one reverses the letters, Rabbi (RB"Y) is *riv* (RY'B) [dispute].[124] This is the Rabbi from the land of Israel, and with him the *Shekhinah* is in conflict.[125]

The relative functions of the halakhists and kabbalists are rendered in terms of the union or estrangement of the primoridal lovers, the Godhead and the *Shekhinah.*

A survey of the relative role of this mysterious author's observations regarding *halakhah* and Kabbalah in overall context seems to support Scholem's understanding, in which rabbinic Judaism retains its legitimacy, yet remains less valid than kabbalistic doctrine. Tishby's arguments seem crushed under the weight of the many relevant allusions in the text, whereas Scholem apparently gleaned the most general tendencies among the profusion of references. One might say that Scholem, like Rabbi Meir, was able to "eat the pomegranate and discard the husk." Scholem's growing preoccupation with the Sabbatean heresy did lead to his repeatedly associating the teachings of the *Ra'aya Meheimna* and *Tiqqunim* with a nascent antinomian sentiment toward rabbinic authority. This tendency is different from the actual renunciation of the commandments. The commandments, as they are presented in the Tannaitic writings with which the Zohar and *Tiqqunim* are meant to be contemporaneous, are not to be questioned or altered.

In methodological terms, Scholem and Baer are overly influenced, in their understandings of the author's relationship to *halakhah,* by the subsequent misuse of the doctrine of the two Torahs by the Sabbateans. A problematic tendency of such historiography is to impute nascent motives into such a text based on the actions of that text's historical interpreters. A phenomenological or literary methodology, as opposed to such a purely historiographical view, holds more promise for the resolution of such contradictory texts in the *Tiqqunim* and *Ra'aya Meheimna.*

Yet the author's own literary methodology was to construct the text according to the associations prevalent in his own stream of consciousness. These associations, and the uses of tropes of the Oral Torah in the *Tiqqunim,* indicate that the language of the law has theurgic meaning. In practice, then, the mundanity of the Oral Torah is still part of the *maskil*'s consciousness, because even the benighted dimension of *Malkhut* is still a realm of great theurgic power.

6

The Theurgic Dimension of the Commandments

There are reasons for *miẓvot* that are not intended to be revealed.

—*Tiqqunei ha-Zohar*, 130b.

Jewish Mysticism is the sum of the attempts made to put a mystical interpretation on the content of Rabbinical Judaism.

—Gershom Scholem[1]

As indicated earlier, the relationship between the *maskil* and the law is ambivalent, to the extent of being perceived as antinomian by mystics and critical scholars alike. In fact, the role of *halakhah* in *Tiqqunei ha-Zohar* and *Ra'aya Meheimna* can be determined through examining the dominant rabbinic motifs cited in these works. The author proposes a theurgic religious practice grounded in theosophical Kabbalah. *Tiqqunei ha-Zohar* and *Ra'aya Meheimna* tend to employ more widespread and sophisticated symbolization of halakhic ideas than the earlier sections of the Zohar.

The law's mystical dimension flows from the mystique of practice, creating new possibilities for religious experience.

Halakhic systems and rhetoric are means of interaction with the hidden functions of the Divine. Religious practice is a means of deepening one's understanding of the hidden and the revealed elements of existence. The practitioner's existential situation is in tension with the origins of the formal rite. Historical distance from the "simple" understanding of the ritual act invokes a mystery, the disjunction of present reality and the transcendent.

The individual laws are metaphors for human and national conditions. The tropes of *halakhah* join biblical references as fuel for the author's flow of symbolic associations. Even the rabbis' social observations were reflective of metaphysical dynamics. Their ethical dicta do not merely describe patterns of religious behavior, but, rather, are insights into the very nature of the adept's condition. Contemplation of the Torah and the practice of the *miẓvot,* particularly prayer, are also vehicles for kabbalistic theurgy.[2]

Tiqqunei ha-Zohar and *Ra'aya Meheimna* assign differing functions to the positive and the negative *miẓvot*. The talmudic dictum "One increases in holiness and one does not decrease" is interpreted as implying that the negative *miẓvot* are secondary to the positive.[3] The positive commandments are symbolized or alluded to in such images as the apotropaic dove's wings,[4] or the Divine glory or *kavod.*[5] Different areas of Jewish law are understood in broadly symbolic terms. For example, the citron of the feast of Tabernacles or the broken *maẓẓah* of the Passover meal are symbols of the *Shekhinah,* as are all references to archetypal femininity. The laws concerning the return of lost property are seen as a metaphor for the restoration of authentic gnosis and the commonwealth.[6] Similarly, the various agricultural tithes symbolize the experience of exile.[7] Finally, the exile is symbolized by the forgotten sheaf lying in the "field," itself an archetypal symbol of the *Shekhinah*.

In the opinion of *Tiqqunei ha-Zohar* and *Ra'aya Meheimna,* a characteristic theurgic act is that which unified the ten *sefirot,* because "the Torah and its precepts are for the sake of unification."[8] All recurrences of the number ten are understood as referring to such theurgic actions. The author associated the ten acts composing the order of ritual sacrifice with the ten declarations through which the world was created.[9] These, in turn, are invoked every week in the ten attendant laws of the ritual benediction over wine.[10] The rabbinic dictum "There is no holiness less than ten" validated the prayer quorum (*minyan*)[11] and the idealized human height of 10 cubits.[12] These speculations on the number ten led to the conclusion that each of the ten *sefirot* contained another set of ten *sefirot.*[13]

Acts of speech have direct bearing on metaphysical reality, because God created the world through speech. Vows and oaths, therefore, derive their force from the nature of this Divine speech. Hence, the metaphysical binding power of vows and oaths derives from the same imperatives that bind God to the covenants with the Patriarchs. Vows are invested with greater power than oaths, because of their different nature. An oath, therefore, which is contingent on corporeal objects, derives from the transient world of temporal existence. A vow, which shapes the future behavior of the person who makes it, is contingent on the eternal world to come.[14]

All religious law necessarily contains aspects of the *sefirah Gevurah,* Divine judgment. The energies of that *sefirah* are applied by the rabbinic court.[15] Biblical forms of execution, for example, encompass the discharge of various aspects of Divine judgment.[16] A corrupt judge is an agent of Samael.[17] The gravity of a sin depends on whether it is tried in the earthly or the supernal *Sanhedrin,* or rabbinical court,[18] because the two courts reflect higher and lower aspects of the *Shekhinah.*[19]

In *Tiqqunei ha-Zohar* and *Ra'aya Meheimna,* halakhic figures and tropes are employed in the associative weave of the *kinnuyim.* These random associations explore the theurgic properties of the *miẓvot.* Three areas of *miẓvot* recur particularly: the *miẓvot* that countered the effects of the incarnate demonic, the theurgic applications of the Temple service, and the *miẓvot* that related directly to the Divine body of God.

Halakhah and the Demonic

In the author's myth of chaos, the creation of the demonic came about through the fall of Adam.[20] This demonic power may be presently incarnate in some demonic social caste,[21] in a spirit such as Samael,[22] or in the energies harbored by the organs of the body and its paradigm in the Divine anthropos.[23] *Tiqqunei ha-Zohar* and *Ra'aya Meheimna* are concerned with the role of *halakhah* in countering the mischief wrought by this malevolent force.

The *miẓvot* serve a purpose that is both protective and restorative. Their most important function is as an instrument in the struggle between the forces of good and evil. The commission of prohibited acts strengthens the forces of demonic chaos:

> Sin does not extinguish the Torah, but sin can extinguish *miẓvah*. A *miẓvah* is a lamp. Whoever commits a sin is really extinguishing his own lamp, of which it says: *The human soul is the lamp of God* (Proverbs 20:27). This extinguishing leaves his own body in darkness. One who draws the *Shekhinah* out of her place darkens and extinguishes that place. This darkness is sin, *a slave-girl who supplants her mistress* (Proverbs 30:23). Redeeming the *miẓvah* from the realm of the unlearned [*ammei ha-areẓ*] extinguishes their lamp, upholding (Samuel I 2:9) *The wicked perish in darkness.* But there is no extinguishing the Masters of the Torah, for they shine with many secrets of the Torah. "Light" ['*or*] is called[24] "*secret*" [*raz*]. And the *miẓvot* of the Torah that the rabbis uphold are the Torah for them, night and day it will not be extinguished for them, for they uphold: *And you will meditate on them day and night* (Joshua 1:8).[25]

The struggle between the holy and the demonic is reflected empirically in the conditions of ritual purity and impurity. The palpability of *tum'ah*, ritual impurity, is apparent in Jewish mysticism as early as the *merkavah* tradition.[26] Medieval philosophers had attempted to qualify the empirical nature of this status.[27] Maimonidean tradition considered *tum'ah* an intellectual construct for the development of human values. The theosophical Kabbalah, however, considered it a source of empirical evil. According to this understanding, a demonic entity inhabits wounded [*tref*] animals. The angel of death rises from between the dying beast's horns and this demonic association is personified in the Tannaitic appellations "goring bull-defiled flesh" (*shor mu'ad basar tame'*):[28] "The sacrifices of Esau, the evil inclination, of which it says: *Let my father sit up and eat of his son's game* (Genesis 27:31)—these are the provisions [*shever*] from the *shevarim,*[29] which are red from the realm of the beast, the ox, fresh meat and pure. And there is another meat, the meat found torn in the field, on which the spirit of impurity rests, the angel of death that rides on the horns of the goring bull, impure meat."[30]

Ritual impurity is fetishized. The gentile meat in the marketplace is not merely forbidden but evil. Contact with it, and indeed with all elements of gentile culture, pollutes and defiles the adept, lowering his spiritual attainment. Nonetheless, meat infested with this spirit is still distinct from the demonic aspect of the sacrifice.

The demonic's rapaciousness is satisfied by aspects of certain sacrifices, the negative commandments, and the agricultural tithes. The scapegoat, the bitter waters of the unfaithful wife, the decapitated calf (Deuteronomy 21:1), the straps and the extra threads of hair in the *tefillin* are also detritus left for demonic forces and "appeasement of the evil eye."[31]

Mixing of neutral quantities renders them demonic. This is the esoteric meaning of the biblical prohibition of the mixing of seed crops (*kilayim*), wool and linen (*sha'atnez*),[32] and grafting fruit trees.[33] The prohibitions of incest and other illicit liaisons are further examples of this illicit mixing. The case of the Tree of Knowledge of Good and Evil is used to exemplify this demonization of mixed neutral quantities. Here, it is compared to the prohibited mixture of wool and linen: "Every *miẓvah* is a fruit-bearing tree, so it says: *le-mino,* "of its kind." But the Tree of the Knowledge of Good and Evil is not *le-mino*; it is mixed with other species, so it says: *Don't sow your field with mixed seeds, nor wear mixtures of wool and linen* (Leviticus 19:19)."[34]

The world exists in a dichotomized condition of good and evil. This is catastrophic, yet worse still is the confusion of these two forces. The interbreeding of species reflects the mythic chaos that encompasses existence. Order exists in the consciousness of the *maskil,* whose religious practice is an instrument for restoring order in the world.

The Motif of Quaternity

The *Heikhalot di-Qedushah,* or "Palaces of Holiness," is a section of the Zohar that details the heavenly palaces that sit at the base of the sefirotic tree.[35] That text seems to associate the biblical forms of execution with the actions of the demonic: "When the Other Side joins with judgment, its accusations reign in the four judicial executions: stoning, burning, the sword, and hanging."

The *Tiqqunim* and *Ra'aya Meheimna* expand on this image, invoking a recurring paradigm of transition from demonic triunity to redemptive quaternity. These include the three years required for a fruit tree to reach maturity, the still small voice[36] that announced Elijah's theophany[37] and the three hapless victims of the expedition into the *pardes.* In kabbalistic terms, these structures signify a process of transition from a demonic triunity to a redemptive quaternity.

The redemptive aspects of quaternity are further portrayed in the widely reproduced study of the four general categories of damages set forth in the Mishnah, the four *avot neziqin.* The talmudic laws of damages are identified with the four beasts that draw the celestial chariot of Ezekiel.[38] The adoption of this theme is a radical re-adaptation of an important and central area of talmudic discourse:[39]

> Rise, *Ra'aya Meheimna,* to set forth the laws of damages in this order HVYH, which is (Psalms 68:18) *God's chariots are myriads upon myriads* that are the ox, eagle, lion, and man. On the right side, the side of YHVH, this is the order of the four beasts: man, lion, eagle, and ox, and according to the differences of the HVYH's are the movement and order of the beasts. The beasts are the other side, the damages of the left, this is their order *SheNA"AN.* Therefore their beginning, the ox, is related with the four major damages, the ox, the pit, the tooth, and the fire, and their conclusion is the suspected man. Rise up, come to life with judgments![40]

The beasts that drew the Divine chariot in Ezekiel 1 are linked to the four central sources of damage, the ox, the pit, the tooth, and the fire. The audible manifestation of God's name in the liturgical *Adonai* results from the realm of judgment, the *sefirah Gevurah,* and its power to exact retribution: "The *Ra'aya Meheimna* began and said: *Open my lips, my Lord, and my mouth will tell your praises* (Psalms 51:17). ADNY (Lord) may be reversed to spell *DINA* (law). Therefore the Masters of the Mishnah said, the law of the *malkhut* is law.[41] All laws are judged with this name."[42]

The quaternity of the chariot symbolizes certain aspects of rabbinic civil law. In each case, the law leads the litigants from the demonic triunity of unrequited sin to the redemptive quaternity of completed judgment. *Gevurah* is particularly indicated by the Divine name ELOHIM:

> A rabbinical court requires three. The rabbinical court is the *Shekhinah.* Three, for the three Patriarchs. The central pillar is the True Judge, who judges from the realm of ADNY. The True Judge is there, and from the realm of the name ELOHIM he judges, as is written (Psalms 75:8): *For Elohim judges.* What judgments are there? One: the judgments of the ox; the second: the judgments of the pit; the third: the judgments of fire; and the fourth: the judgments of man.[43]

The rabbinical court of three is the agent of *Gevurah.* The judgment and punishment are purgative; when the judgment is carried out, the practitioner is spared further punishment. Beyond the four main families of damages, various halakhic constructs in civil law are presented as further instances of purgative judgment through redemptive quaternity:

> The laws of the four guardians, he who guards without payment, with payment, the borrower, and the leaser, correspond to four judgments: the law of the divisions between partners, laws of division of land, the laws of slaves and maidservants, and the laws of litigants in all kinds of litigations, which may involve financial responsibility, theft, and loss, or the case of one who injures his neighbor and kills him, through one of the four legal executions.[44]

The agents of judgment for the transgression of commandments are demonic forces. The job of judging the wicked is ceded to these elements. This force is the shadow aspect of the *Shekhinah,* the "wicked maidservant": "Master, the Blessed Holy One is ADNY, judging all kinds of judgments for the evil maidservant *that supplants her mistress* (Proverbs 30:23), who generates all damages, the agents of damages. The souls of the wicked are, as the Masters of the Mishnah taught: 'the damages in the world.'[45] A false deity, a demon, thief, sinner, and his spouse, the elixir of death."[46]

The four reparations of damages[47] are then invoked as the effects of the mischief of the demonic *Shekhinah:*

> Damages, disability, shame, and healing for the *Shekhinah* and her children. Disability: the neglect of Torah, causing her to neglect her children. Healing: with words of Torah.[48] Damages: the mischief of the angels of destruction, rage and anger. Shame: for they shamed the *Shekhinah* with idolatry, lying, and saying *Where is your God?* (Psalms 42:4). Many thefts are committed by the evil maidservant, as it says: *The robbery of the poor in your houses* (Isaiah 3:14). The evil maidservant steals many blessings from the *Shekhinah,* through harsh taxes and many harsh laws that are enacted against the children, and many sacrifices in the Temple from which the *Matronita* was deprived.[49]

The demonic feminine precipitates the supreme indignity, stripping the *Shekhinah* of the priestly vestments, which had been painstakingly created through the artisanship of the *maskilim* and their mystical exegeses of the Torah: "And shame, of the *Matronita,* who was left naked, deprived of the four golden garments, which shine from the four stone mountains with twelve gems, diamonds, [deprived of] the jacket, with bells and pomegranates, [deprived of] the four white garments, which the *Matronita* used to wear for the King, as it says: *You will see it as a reminder of an eternal covenant* (Genesis 9:16). She stole many sacrifices from her mistress."[50]

Having presented the negative feminine, the author is obliged to portray the male aspect of the demonic. This aspect is incarnate in the goring bull, the subject of much case law in the *halakhot* of damages:

> The goring bull: her husband entered the Palace, his master, with his four sources of damages, which are iniquity, destruction, anger, and rage, which are all liable to destroy. With his body he tramples the vessels, the altar, menorah, table, and its implements. He tramples and breaks them, with his tooth he eats all the sacrifices of the foods of the table *that crushed and stamped the remains* (Daniel 7:19), crumbling everything and *the remains:* these are the entrails and fats and grain offerings. *He stamped:* with his horn he killed the Priests and Levites, destroying everything, *he brought low the kingdom and its ministers* (Lamentations 2:2).[51]

The fourth source of damages, the pit, is portrayed as the devouring vaginal abyss of the demonic feminine. This havoc wrought by this demonic entity is portrayed in terms of the humbling of the city Jerusalem as portrayed in the book of Lamentations:

> The pit is the evil feminine, Lilit. In her house, a prison, the evil maidservant seized the *Matronita* and her children in exile and bound them in chains and ropes, and her children's hands are bound behind them. *She sits among the nations and finds no rest* (Lamentations 1:3), and what is more, *all her suitors have shamed her, for they saw her nakedness, so she sighs and turns aside* (Ibid. 1:8) Also the prostitute, the blazing fire: *A fire has been set in Zion* (Ibid. 4:11). After that, the worthless sinner rises, the fourth, of whom it says: *A man is always suspect.*[52] Whether asleep or awake he sets his livestock loose, and he eats and destroys and tramples the vineyards and orchards of Jerusalem, destroying everything.[53]

The civil laws that are the basis of talmudic inquiry address the inner nature of the demonic. The four sources of damages are earthly manifestations of demonic powers, portraying social chaos. The rabbinical court adjudicates these catastrophes at the same time as it punishes the wicked, through the harshness of Divine judgment. This spiritualization of the Talmud's four manners of execution[54] also corresponds to the four letters YHVH.[55]

Wheat, Chaff, and Circumcision

Wheat has been an important and evocative image in Jewish symbolism from Canaanite times. *Tiqqunei ha-Zohar* continues the Zohar's symbolization of wheat and chaff, fine flour and rough flour as metaphors for the dimensions of the Torah.[56] In these well-known expositions, the author of the Zohar refers to the exoteric Torah as its straw and untithed produce (*teven* and *tevel*). The Zohar's classical comparison equated the rabbinic mentality with eating the straw of the Torah, the inedible detritus.

Tiqqunei ha-Zohar and *Ra'aya Meheimna* apply this motif to the sociological typologies of the author's day. The rabbinic authorities of the day are as "the donkeys of Torah who eat the straw of Torah."[57] These "cattle" are, in turn, attached to *qelippah*, or "husk."[58] The *erev rav* are also chaff and straw, *se'or ve-ḥameẓ,* yeast and dough, whereas the community of Israel, a euphemism for the *Shekhinah,* is the *solet nekiyah,* fine flour:

> From the realm of produce, the five kinds of bread, broken off from all, and they are wheat, barley, oat, corn, and spelt. These are compared to Israel: *Israel is holy to God, the first fruits of God's produce* (Jeremiah 2:3). When they came out of the Exile, they were broken, until the food was sorted out from the detritus, the chaff and straw, the mixed multitude. . . . Until they were separated out, the *Yud,* the tithe, did not dwell on the *Hey,* the bread, made of the five types of grain as it says: *Hand upon the throne of the Lord* (Exodus 17:16).[59] So the chaff and the straw do not require tithing until they have been separated. . . . Just as wheat that has been cleaned is brought to the storehouse, so the purified Israel are brought to Jerusalem, the mountain of God, as it says (Psalms 24:3): *Who will come to the mountain of God, and who will rise up in His holy place? He who has clean hands and a pure heart . . .*[60]

The mystic discards and deprecates the exoteric aspect of the Torah. According to the *halakhah,* chaff and straw are not subject to tithes, and so the *maskilim* throw them away: "These are the cattle, who only know the Torah's chaff, the outer shell, the straw, of which it says, 'straw and chaff are excused from tithing.' For the scholars of Torah, the masters of the secrets, throw the straw and chaff away and consume the Torah's inner kernel. The twenty-two letters of the Torah come to the sum *ḥitah* [wheat] . . ."[61]

The search for the essence of the law is compared to sifting flour. The mixed multitude are the result of the incomplete sifting of the "flour" that symbolizes the people Israel:

> There are two husks (*qelippin*), green and white, for the husks of the nut, one is *tohu,* the green line, while the second is *bohu,* polished stones,[62] a strong husk, like a polished stone. These correspond to the two husks, the chaff and straw of the wheat. The third, thin husk, corresponds to the bran that clings to the wheat and must be ground in a mill to separate it, like the grinding of a man's mouth. So one must savor the words of the Torah, sifting the impurities, the bran, through his lips until he determines the *halakhah,* the fine flour.[63]

This motif of sifting wheat originates in the tradition of chaos as the underlying theme of reality. *Tiqqunei ha-Zohar* draws on the rabbinic tradition that the instrument of the fall, the "fruit," was a kernel of wheat. The tithe *ḥallah,* the apportionment of dough to the Temple, atones for the fall. Therefore it is incumbent on women, who must necessarily atone for Eve's complicity in the fall: "For her sake Adam, the *ḥallah* of the world, died. So she must take *ḥallah* out of her dough, for it is her drop of seed that she returns to Adam."[64]

Because the fall is sexual in nature, the chaff and straw of the wheat are compared to the foreskin, in that each serves the demonic *qelippah*'s functions and purposes.[65] Each motif requires the peeling away of barriers to the Divine. *Tiqqunei ha-Zohar* understands entrance into the covenant of circumcision as transition from the realm of the demonic into that of the holy.[66] The removal of the demonic detritus leaves the "sign of the covenant," which takes its place together with the Sabbath and the *mezuzah* as windows into the realm of the higher *sefirot*.[67] The tradition that the righteous are often born circumcized underscores the demonic nature of the foreskin.[68]

The transition from the demonic to the holy is accomplished through the stripping away of the husk or *qelippah* inherent in the three actions of circumcision, *'orele, peri'ah,* and *'atifu de-dama,* the cutting of the foreskin, uncovering the corona, and the drawing off of the ensuing flow of blood. *'Orele* and *peri'ah* are synonymous with various demonic pairs: Samael and the serpent, or Rome and Constantinople.[69] Each aspect of the act constitutes a bribe for the demonic: "The flow of blood from the *peri'ah* will save you from the pressure of the grave, because it gives food to the murderer, sixteen sword edges for the sword of the Blessed Holy One for *milah, peri'ah, meẓiẓa,* and the thirteen covenants."[70]

These layers of *qelippah* are likened to the three shells of the *egoz,* the classical expression of the hiddenness of the Divine. Circumcision is a transition from demonic triunity to redemptive quaternity, which is symbolized by the sign of the covenant: "The *membrum virile* has three coverings, like the shells of the nut, *tohu va-vohu* [primordial chaos] . . . the first *qelippah: vohu* . . . the second *qelippah,* and *hoshekh* [darkness], the third *qelippah,* as it says: 'One does not explain matters of illicit sexuality in groups of three.' "[71]

After the circumcision, the foreskin is hidden in a pile of earth, with this explanation:

> Rabbi Eliezer said, "Father, what is the secret meaning of the covenant, in that we bury the foreskin in a vessel of earth?" He said to him, "My son, I once asked the same thing of Elijah [the prophet]. . . . He told me that the foreskin is the spouse of the primordial serpent that brought death to Adam and to all creation, so we prepare it a vessel of earth, which is its sustenance, as it says: *The serpent's bread is dust* (Isaiah 65:25). So it separates from human beings . . . and this dust is like the dust of the altar, of which it says: *Make me an altar of earth* (Exodus 20:24)."[72]

In societal terms, circumcision symbolizes the eventual stripping away of the lower, debased dimension of the covenant. As ideal religious practice removes the garments of the *Shekhinah* to facilitate Divine union, so circumcision strips away the foreskin, or barrier, between Israel and the transcendent law:

> The eighth day is the sign of the holy pillar, the eighth of all levels, and the circumcison of that pillar removes the foreskin from the covenant, for at that time the holy people remove the foreskin from the covenant. The Blessed Holy One gathers all His hosts and is revealed, truly removing that foreskin above from the covenant of the holy pillar. All the actions of Israel below arouse an action above, so at that time, the foreskin is removed from all the holy people from above.[73]

Like the blood offered in sacrifice,[74] the blood of circumcision unifies the adherent with the highest levels of the Divine, saving the adherent from the Angel of Death.[75] Circumcision is a metaphor for an eschatological understanding of the transformation of the nature of Divine law and religious experience. The *maskil* must strip away the barriers to perception, clarifying the legalists' obfuscations by stripping away the corporeal shells that obscure the Divine. The symbolism of circumcision is not arbitrary. The *membrum virile,* the point at which being is passed on, is marked with the sign of the revelation of God.

Theurgy and the Anthropos

In the deepest recesses of the Zohar's esotericism lies the the ancient notion of God the anthropos, with the human literally created in the Divine image. The texts in the Zohar that delineate the anthropomorphic structure of the Divine are the most theologically brazen, and they provide the key to understanding many oblique Zoharic exegeses. The editors of the classical editions of the Zohar showed great discretion with regard to this tradition and were apt to append lengthy disclaimers and apologies to it.[76]

The *Idrot,* those passages of the Zohar that boldly delineate the secrets of the Divine anthropos, are saturated with messianic longing.[77] Both modern scholars and Lurianic theorists considered them to be the culminating texts of the Zohar.

One may trace the interactions of thirteenth-century kabbalists according to their awareness of the *Idrot*; the systematic presentations of Cordovero and Luria are likewise much indebted to those texts. Both Scholem and Tishby considered the *Idrot* a catalyst for Moshe de Leon's creative muse.[78] Yehuda Liebes has qualified the image of the main part of the Zohar as the work of a single author, yet he too has demonstrated the development of the *Idrot* to be the central preoccupation of the same circles that produced the Zohar.[79] The *Idrot* are suffused with the realization of ultimate metaphysical truths, not least because they end with the ecstatic deaths of several of the adepts of Shimon Bar Yoḥai's circle. The *Tiqqunim,* as well, are preoccupied with the *Idrot,* in which the interplay of the *sefirot* corresponds to the contours of a Divine anthropos.

The paradigm for the most transcendent levels of Divinity is the primordial man, *Adam Qadmon.* This anthropos serves as a metaphor for God, the Cosmos, the Torah,[80] and by association, the Temple and its sacrificial cult.[81] *Tiqqunei ha-Zohar* interprets the anthropos teachings as forming a response to humankind's present dilemma. Interaction with the Divine is possible through projecting the Divine anthropos onto the human model. Specific rituals begin this transformation and repair the wounded body of the universe.

The anthropos paradigm expresses the hierarchical nature of the *sefirot.* It also illustrates the dichotomy of the body and the soul, for transition down the sefirotic hierarchy requires a similarly radical transition from dimension to dimension.[82] This same relationship is a paradigm for the effluence of Divinity into the corporeal world.[83] Contemplative mystical experience, in introspective withdrawal into the soul, is the medium for ascent into the highest dimensions of the universe:[84] "R. Eliezer said, 'Father, how is man made in the Divine image, for we have heard many opinions?' He said to him, 'My son, when all the *sefirot* were made they were included in the image of the soul, and the soul was their vehicle.' "[85]

The soul's levels mirror the levels of religious expression. The *miẓvah* is symbolic of the *nefesh,* or lower soul, whereas the Torah represents the *ruaḥ,* or emotive soul.[86] Every intermediate level of the soul interlocks with a higher level, until they reach the source of the transcendent element in the human soul, the Divine throne: "[Jacob's] ladder is the living soul, the throne of the name YHVH, which is the awe and the love, the Torah and the *mizvah* dwelling in it. From this throne are hewn all the souls of Israel. Its image is the human face."[87]

The practitioner's every limb relates to a specific *sefirah.*[88] The practice of the *mizvot* draws the Divine into the adept's very limbs:[89] "Rabbi Eliezer said to him 'But haven't we learned that there is no body above?' He said to him, 'My son, in the world to come, there will be a transcendent mother, but this world has the *Shekhinah*'s body.' This body is the Torah, from which hang all of the *mizvot.*"[90]

In the Divine macrocosm, the limbs of the Divine anthropos are bedecked with *mizvot* as fruit hangs from a tree:

> All the *mizvot* are contingent on the King's image. *Mizvot* that are for a reward are contingent on that higher servant.[91] One must understand that all the *mizvot* are in the image of the king. Some are contingent on the head, and some on the eyes. Many angels and servants, the eyes of God, are assigned to them. There are *mizvot* that are contingent on the ears, with attendant angels who are called *ears of God.* There are *mizvot* that are called the face, with attendant angels called *face of God,* of whom it says: *Four faces for one* (Ezekiel 1:6). There are *mizvot* that are contingent on the nose, with attendant angels, of whom it says: *He makes his angels into breaths* (Psalms 104:4). There are *mizvot* that are contingent on the mouth, and angels assigned to the voices and words of Torah, concerning which it says: *For the bird of heaven will lead the voice, and the winged one will tell the matter* (Ecclesiastes 10:20). There are *mizvot* that are contingent on the hands of the king, with attendant angels that are called hands, as it says: *A man's hands were under their wings* (Ezekiel 1:8). There are *mizvot* that hang like grapes in a cluster. . . . There are *mizvot* that hang from the sign of the covenant, with attendant angels who are called the *Masters of Signs,* of whom it says *They shall be for signs* (Genesis 1:14). And similarly it says of Moses: *This is a sign for you* (Exodus 3:12). This is the sign to which all the host of heaven are assigned. There are *mizvot*

that are contingent on the feet, with attendant angels, of whom it says: *And the beasts scurried back and forth . . . and their feet were straight feet* (Ezekiel 1:14). They hang from the body like hair, every hair is like an angel hanging from the head. . . . Happy is the soul that is in the image of its master and upholds these *miẓvot!*[92]

The adept nourishes or impoverishes his spiritual body through his actions, be they the performance of *miẓvot* or the commission of transgressions. Sin causes a rupture or a blemish in the Divine body, so that "whoever violates a *miẓvah* . . . defiles the image of the King."[93] Similarly, the fulfillment of positive precepts nourish the human and divine anthropos. By virtue of their spiritual perfection, the righteous embody the synthesis of the physical and the transcendent, so that "their *miẓvot* are engraved on their bones."[94] The same is true for transgressors of the law: "Skin (*'or*) was Adam's garment. If he was good it was light (*or*), the hidden light for the righteous,[95] and if he was wicked, it was the skin of the serpent, made of the four elements, and the negative *miẓvot* that people transgress, as the Masters of the Mishnah said, 'A man's sins are engraved on his bones.' "[96]

The association of the cosmos with the body underlies the rabbinic dictum that "every *ẓaddik* has a world of his own."[97] The *miẓvot* are a soteric agency for the redemption of the cosmos and the individual practitioner's state. The motif of the anthropos creates an identity between the adept and the universe.

Sacrifice

The Zohar,[98] *Tiqqunim,* and *Ra'aya Meheimna* portray sacrifice as the most profound theurgic act in the synchrony of the anthropomorphic images of God, the universe, and the adept. Temple sacrifices are an overt exchange of spiritual energy. The immolation of the animal's body processes and cycles Divine and demonic energies. The author of the *Tiqqunim* idealized the Temple cult and viewed it as an esoteric rite. Such idealization of the cult's abattoir-like reality was, in large part, due to psychic and historical distance from that institution.

The Tabernacle itself was an earthly microcosm of the universe; to ponder its constituent elements was to ponder the divine superstructure.[99] Moreover, the structure of the Temple also conforms to the microcosm of the Divine body.[100] Every aspect of the Temple's function, such as the priestly blessings and duties or the Levitical night watches, is portrayed in terms of its metaphysical dimensions.[101]

The soteric function of the Temple sacrifices is explained in terms of the interaction of the *sefirot.*[102] Sin causes a rupture in the Divine body, which is assuaged by the body of the sacrifice. The immolation of the sacrificial animal redeems the limbs of the human body. This action links the worshipper to the limbs of the *Shekhinah,*[103] for "sacrifices atone for a person's limbs, according to the sins that are contingent on that limb."[104] The grandeur of the cult is portrayed in mythic terms:

> In the future the Blessed Holy One will unsheath the sun, the righteous will be healed with it. A fiery lion will come from the Throne of Judgment to consume the sacrifices. These are assigned to each limb with which one sins, each a nemesis, as had been taught "he who does one sin acquires one nemesis."[105] When this Divine fire comes down and ignites those limbs and fats and descends like a fiery lion, it will ignite the demons that are assigned to them, and absolve the sins of Israel, the limbs of the *Shekhinah.*[106]

The sacrifice is the point of interaction between the lower *sefirot* and the mundane realm. Trangressions remove the sinner from the natural order, but sacrifice returns him, satiating the four beasts and deflecting their destructive proclivities.[107] With these beasts mollified, the energies of the sacrifice can ascend into the higher realms of the Divine. Once again, redemptive quaternity must be attained for the religious act to be accepted:

> There are four beasts on the throne: lion, ox, eagle, and man. The human body has four elements, from them come

the four beasts that make up the soul. The soul is sustained by four. When a person sins with one of the four elements, it is as if he sinned with his soul. So it is written: *When he sins in a soul* (Numbers 6:11). At that time, the water separates from the fire, the wind from the dust. From the dust come seeds to sustain man, from the water come the animals that sustain the lion, from fire come the grazing animals to sustain the ox, and from wind come birds that sustain the eagle. When a person sins, these elements separate violently. The name of God departs and is replaced by the evil inclination, Samael, Satan. God does not dwell in separation, as it says: *They divided their hearts and they will be guilty* (Hosea 10:2). Sacrifices must come from that aspect with which they sinned, to unify[108] the four elements that have been separated. When they reunify, the Blessed Holy One descends upon them and Satan flees, rather than be immolated in the sacrificial fire.[109]

The Zohar and *Tiqqunim* clarified the Torah's bewildering differentiation of the sacrifices. *The korban oleh ve-yored,* or the "rising and descending sacrifice,"[110] follows the descent of the higher *Shekhinah* to the lower. As these two aspects of the *Shekhinah* unite, the practitioner is included in their union. This movement equates the transformative aspect of the Divine feminine, *Imma 'Ila'ah,* the "highest Mother," with the elementary, erotic, and unitive aspect.[111] The sacrifices reassume their primitive identity as God's food; their immolation, like the song of the Levites, evokes the ascent to the Divine.[112]

Various sacrificial traditions have different theurgic functions. The burnt offering, *'olah,* represents the quality of mercy, which catalyzes and dissipates the force of Judgment through the sin offering.[113] The *menorah* evokes the *Shekhinah* as an instrument of unification.[114]

Every sacrifice has an aspect that may be devoted to the realm of the demonic.[115] Some sacrifices, such as the guilt offering, are clearly a bribe to the demonic.[116] *Minḥah,* the humble grain offering, is specifically brought to "break the anger of Samael."[117]

The *temidim,* or ongoing regimen of sacrifices, represent the constancy of God. Just as the sefirotic tree is one entity with multiple functions, so the various *temidim* have different functions on various Sabbaths and Holy Days: "All the *temidin* are attributes of the Blessed Holy One . . . and even though all the *sefirot* are as one, even so, every *sefirah* governs various Sabbaths, and seasons, and holidays. The attribute that rules over a specific time contains all the other *sefirot.* They are called by that attribute . . . "[118]

Sheḥitah, ritual slaughter, is the greatest agent of transformation. Sacrificial slaughter must take place at the north side of the Temple, because the qualities of Divine Judgment are associated with the north.[119] The laws attending the slaughter are reinterpreted kabbalistically so that such repetitive formulas as the twelve examinations of the knife,[120] or the five disqualifications in the act of slaughter,[121] are imbued with metaphysical significance. Ritual slaughter is also a metaphor for human death.[122] Fish and locusts, which do not require slaughter, are reincarnated scholars. At their deaths, these spiritual elect are simply gathered to the Divine, as fish are killed by merely being gathered into the fisherman's net. They never feel the knife of Divine Judgment, the untimely cessation of their lives by virtue of their accumulated sins.[123]

The Zohar contains many statements regarding the proper *kavvanah* or intention attendant upon sacrifices.[124] The author of the *Tiqqunim* goes further, reinterpreting the Maimonidean critique of the cult, which implies that the physical sacrifice is to be transcended in a more enlightened age.[125] *Tiqqunei ha-Zohar* and *Ra'aya Meheimna* portray this transcendence in terms of a hierarchy of intentions based on the development of the sacrificer's consciousness. The flawed practice of the ignorant is merely a bribe for the demonic, while the simple pietists can offer only their prayers and good deeds. The *maskilim* offer their esoteric practice as a sacrifice.[126] This typology makes an implicit critique of those who "consume" the Torah at the level of simple (*peshat*) exegesis.[127] The individual gives his or her essence to God, and it is altogether clear that some essences are intrinsically superior to others.

Sacrificial Organs

The limbs are sealed in the secret of sacrifice . . .

—Zohar III 235b

Bodies not only reflect the glory their souls receive in God's presence but are also the place where persons are rewarded and punished in their specificity . . .

—Caroline Bynum[128]

The association of the *mizvot* with the sacrifice extends to the effects on the adept's spiritual and physical bodies. The animal's organs are counterparts of organs in the Divine anthropos as well as the organs that are nourished or abused by the practice or abrogation of the *mizvot*. This comparison of the elements of the sacrificial body and the Divine body makes extensive use of medieval theories of medicine, elevated to an esoteric level. The sacrifice is a cathartic moment of unification between the worshipper's body and the Divine anthropos. It restores and sanctifies the limbs that have been damaged through sin. There is a radical implication that the sacrifice empowers the dormant strength of the Divine body.[129]

The Divine anthropos circulates holy and demonic energies in the same way that the body circulates air and fluids. The *sefirot* are also understood as conduits for this exchange of energies. The lungs are the conduit for the *ruah*, or spirit, the seat of existence. The dynamism of the breath evokes the functions of the Divine effluence: "The heart is the seat of judgment. The four beasts are the heart's messengers and the two chambers of the lungs and the two kidneys. *And their faces and wings were separated above* (Ezekiel 1:11) to receive the King, which is (Isaiah 11:2) *a spirit*[130] *of wisdom and understanding, a spirit of counsel and power, a spirit of consciousness and awe of the Lord.*[131]

The theurgic effects of the sacrifices are concentrated in the organs that filter the body's impurities. The biological forces that regulate those organs have counterparts in the cosmos just as their mundane function is to catch impurities in the body, so their cosmic function is to be a receptacle for the extraneity of the demonic.[132] The toxicity of the bile, for instance, is compared to "the sword of the Angel of Death."[133] The liver is compared to the leather strap of the *tefillin*, a classic symbol of the demonic.[134] The fats and entrails are an atonement for the sins of the body, that the practitioner's soul not be consumed by *Geihinnom*.[135] The consumption of the organs by the forces of the Divine or the demonic is rendered in the mythic imagery of the lion of holiness and the dog of the demonic:

> The heart is the altar, on which is the sacrificial blood, of which it says: *You will sacrifice on it* (Exodus 20:24). If they are worthy, the lion descends to eat the sacrifice, and if they are not [worthy] a dog descends. Where? Onto the liver and the bile, *Geihinnom*, the leech with two daughters, crying "Give! Give!"[136] like the dog's bark, the double-edged sword of the Angel of Death . . . of which it says: *Its end is bitter*[137] *as wormwood, sharp as a double-edged sword* (Proverbs 5:4). The liver is Samael, the bile is its poison. When the bile rules the veins and they are overcome with sin, it says of them: *They came to Marah and were unable to drink the waters, for they were bitter* (Exodus 15:23). At that time the veins of the heart are blocked, like Noah, his wife, children, animals, beasts, and birds hidden in the ark. And the heart is blocked, for if the bile extends to the heart, one immediately dies. The bile cannot overcome Israel, who are the heart, except through sin. If they repent, taking on the pure soul of the highest *Shekhinah*, the heart and its arteries are saved, as it says: *And the waters were sweetened* (ibid.).[138]

These organs are symbolized by members of the patriarchal family, which themselves relate to various *sefirot*:

> The liver is Esau, Edom, gathering all the blood, clear or murky, not distinguishing or separating good and bad. The heart is Israel, which distinguishes between good and evil, between pure blood and impure blood, taking only the clearest and cleanest, as one who separates food from waste.[139] After the heart, Jacob, takes the purest blood above, then the liver, Esau, is left with the refuse, which angers him. This is *Geihinnom*, created on the second day, the death of the multi-

> tudes, the evil feminine, strange fires, hard labor. It is called idolatry, for anger comes from it. And from it comes anger to the liver, as the Rabbis taught: *Whoever is angry commits idolatry.*[140] the limb's burning fevers of all the limbs come from the gall. It lights torches in the veins of the liver, threatening to envelope the whole body, like the angry sea, whose waves rise to heaven, threatening to break their bounds and shatter the world . . .[141]

A particularly cathartic role is assigned to the spleen, bile, and liver as receptacles for demonic detritus. For example, the demonic quality of the guilt offering is discernible in the liver, which is "dirty with the sins of Israel,"[142] and the spleen.[143] A characteristic object of these meditations is the demonization of the *sirkhot,* or lesions on the lungs:

> Like the *sirkhot,* which impede the lungs from inflating, so the sins of Israel fuse with the wings of the *Shekhinah* that are the beasts of the throne, so that they cannot rise on the merits of Israel to the Blessed Holy One. They detain her and weigh on her wings, each beast weighed with these sins.[144] The guilt offering is the mother of the mixed multitude, *sirkhah,* holding on to the throne of the *Matronita,* forbidding her to escape from exile. And her merits, which expedite her escape, remain suspended in the air, like a *sirkhah.* This is the central pillar, the contingent guilt offering . . .[145]

In mythic terms, the demonic nature of the *sirkhot* is a manifestation of Lilit, "the evil maidservant, mother of the mixed multitude."[146] Thus the *sirkhot* and liver perform the same functions of intercession and atonement as the scapegoat, which carries off the sins of Israel.[147] Like the guilt and sin offerings, the *sirkhot* provide sustenance for the demonic. By inhibiting the breathing capacity, the *sirkhot* actually inhibit the flow of the Divine channels: "Negative commandments are like refuse, like birds caught in a trap, like the *sirkhot* that do not allow the folds of the lungs to move."[148]

Tiqqunei ha-Zohar counts eighteen possible *sirkhot,* a numbering that entered subsequent exoteric *halakhah.*[149] Whether or not this understanding originated with the author of the *Tiqqunim,* it subsequently affected Rabbi Joseph Caro's seminal commentary *Beit Yosef* [150] in its counting of eighteen *sirkhot.* Later halakhic development created more and more stringencies surrounding the *sirkhot,* so that today an animal with *sirkhot* on its lungs will be rejected out of hand for consumption. Whether or not this growing stringency regarding *sirkhot* derives directly from kabbalistic doctrines remains to be assessed. Although this issue awaits definitive analysis, it may provide an example of a kabbalistic imposition on *halakhah.*

Lulav and Etrog

Four species of vegetation are brought to the worship service on the Sukkot holiday: the myrtle, willow, palm shoot, and citron.[151] The *Tiqqunim* and *Ra'aya Meheimna* interpret in terms of the Divine anthropos. The anthropomorphic metaphor is presented in terms of the rabbinic character of this *miẓvah:*

> The *etrog* is the *Shekhinah,* the heart, the essence of the limbs of the body, which are the myrtle, the palm and the two willow branches. The heart is in the center, and the rest of the limbs surround it. Because of this, the *etrog* is the *Shekhinah,* as the Masters of the Mishnah taught:[152] *if its stem has been removed, or if it has been blemished, it is unfit.* For it must be like the *Shekhinah,* of whom it says: *You are completely beautiful, my bride, there is no blemish in you* (Song of Songs 4:7). The palm branches, that is the *lulav,* of which it says:[153] *If the leaves have split off, it is unfit.* This is cutting the shoots, for isn't the *lulav* the knot that binds all? Whoever blesses it on the first day of Sukkot, it is the knot of unity of everything, *Ḥai olamim*[154] for the eighteen vertebrae in the spine. Therefore the Masters of the Mishnah taught: *the lulav resembles the spine.* The secret meaning of the *lulav* is (Psalms 92:13) *the righteous shall flourish like a palm.*[155]

The act of gathering all the species involves the ingathering of all the forces of the cosmic anthropos. This is particularly the case when the adherent prays with the *lulav:*

> One must shake [the *lulav*] eighteen times in six directions: *He sealed the east in YH"V. . . .* Six times HVY, eighteen letters, all implied in the Book of Formation[156] in six realms. Therefore the Masters of the Mishnah taught:[157] *Move it back and forth, to He to whom the four winds belong, up and down to He to whom the heavens and earth belong.* Three myrtles, the body and the two arms, corresponding to the eye and the two eyelids. Two willow branches, corresponding to the two thighs, and the two lips. When they are brought together with the palm, the backbone . . . they make up the four species of the Divine Chariot, with YHVH riding on them.[158]

The myrtle has a triune nature, which invokes the three Patriarchs, paradigms of the intermediate *sefirot Ḥesed, Din,* and *Tif'eret.* The two willow branches invoke *Neẓaḥ* and *Hod.* The palm shoot, or *lulav,* symbolizes *Tif'eret,* whereas the *etrog,* or citron, symbolizes *Malkhut.* Holding the *lulav* and *etrog* together is an act of unification, symbolizing the union of the transcendent and the corporeal.

The *lulav* is shaken eighteen times.[159] This action, like the eighteen blessings of prayer, relates to the eighteen vertebrae of the backbone.[160] Because the *lulav* is symbolic of the Divine backbone, any fracture in its structure renders it unfit for use. Such a fracture parallels that of gnostic heresy through the images of *kiẓẓuẓ* and *perud,* rupture and separation.[161] The *lulav* and petitional prayer are ways of meditatively imaging the Divine. The anthropomorphic hierarchy of the *sefirot* is invoked in the Divine names that describe them :

> For all blessings, one must bow with the eighteen vertebrae, as the Masters of the Mishnah established, with *until all the vertebrae of the spine bend.*[162] This is for the eighteen blessings that are included in the eighteen worlds. The spine is the *lulav;* if it splits, it is unfit.[163] Therefore, one mustn't interrupt the eighteen blessings of prayer that signify the eighteen shakings of the *lulav.* As the Masters of the Mishnah taught:[164] *Even when a serpent is coiled around your heel, there must not be an interruption.* For there are eighteen worlds unifying YHVH and ADNY. Therefore, YAHDVNHY has the same numerical sum as AMeN. Therefore, *even when a serpent is coiled around*

> *your heel, there must be no interruptions.* When one bows at *Barukh,* it has been learned,[165] *For a scorpion one may interrupt,* for it was taught:[166] *You will live by them and not die by them.* Also,[167] *when bowing, bow at Barukh* one must include in it the ten *sefirot* that are YU"D He"i VA"V He"i.[168]

The spherical *etrog* is held in the left hand, in line with the heart, invoking the wholeness of the paradigmatic figures Jacob and Solomon.[169] The *etrog* has the same aroma as the citron tree from which it comes,[170] indicating the immanence of the Tree of Life in the realm of the Tree of Knowledge. The rabbinic injunction, stipulating that the *etrog* must be the size of an egg,[171] associates the *etrog* with the mythic archetype of the World Egg.[172]

According to these kabbalistic interpretations, the symbols of the *Sukkot* festival celebrate the descent of Divine effluence. The *sukkah* itself represents the sanctified inner realm of the holy. The *lulav* and *etrog* are instruments of the adherent's union with the supernal dimensions of the anthropos. In *Tiqqunei ha-Zohar* and *Ra'aya Meheimna,* the *halakhah* provides nuances for the illumination of the theurgic act.

The Temple cult's importance only magnifies the desolation wrought in its loss, so that a gnawing eschatological pathos haunts these theurgic mysteries. In light of the eventual absence of the sacrificial cult and its soteric effects, this practice is important, placing social pressure on the *maskilim,* whose practice is conducted at the highest level. Certain rituals have the esoteric function of unifying the Divine anthropos and, thence, of repairing the damage wrought by the chaotic nature of existence. The Sabbath, especially, provides a respite from this same struggle, and its palliative effects extend over the entire week. The *maskil*'s low state was alleviated by his understanding of the law's theurgic power to resolve the unredeemed state of existence.

7

Agencies of Unification: The Sabbath and Prayer

Theosophical Kabbalah understood certain *miẓvot* as particularly concentrating and centering the effluence of Divine energies. Other *miẓvot* protect the individual from malevolent or demonic forces. Reigious practice consists of balancing these two kinds of *miẓvot* to counter and take advantage of the shifting effects of the Divine.

Medieval Jewish philosophers identified the consciousness of God's unity, *miẓvat ha-yiḥud,* as a specific commandment of the Torah. To have this consciousness might be an actual act of "unification," or it might be merely a *kavvanah* or intention to be assumed in the course of one's practice. In the *Tiqqunim,* unification with the Divine is a positive act that takes place through the contemplative practice of certain *miẓvot.*

The Sabbath

The Zohar displays a subtle understanding of the metaphysical rhythms of time. The cycles of the day, week, and year are portrayed as a garment for the unfolding of the Divine effluence. The continuum of time is a step down from the unchanging essence of the supernal Godhead.[1] The charged metaphysical nature of the Sabbath is reflected in the halakhic strictures that attend its observance.[2] The Sabbath is a day free of creation, the day that "the *Shekhinah* is freed from her exile."[3] Hence, its prohibitions derive from withdrawal from constructive actions.[4]

Tiqqunei ha-Zohar emphasizes the theurgic aspects of the thirty-nine actions forbidden on the Sabbath. These actions derive directly from the catastrophe of the fall, as they encompass the curses made upon Adam at the expulsion from Eden: "When the dew[5] reigns, the sages forbade the thirty-nine forbidden actions, which are called *avot melakhot*,[6] corresponding to the Patriarchs on whom reigns the dew which is thirty-nine. Of these thirty-nine actions, ten were inflicted on Adam, ten on Eve, ten on the serpent, and nine on the land. Since this dew already reigns on the Sabbath, no lashes are administered on the Sabbath."[7]

Because the *halakhah* defined these actions as paradigmatic acts of creation, they are essential to corporeal existence. On the Sabbath, when the Divine effluence flows directly into the corporeal world, one must refrain from them. Refraining from these actions reflects the *Shekhinah's* tranquility on the Sabbath day. On the Sabbath, humankind has no complaint with the state of creation, so that one is forbidden to interfere with it: "Wherever Israel are, they are protected and tranquil. Therefore it is forbidden to plow the earth and to make furrows, for it is like a blemish in the Holy Land, the *Shekhinah*. Therefore it is forbidden to use agricultural tools on the Sabbath, even to carry a stone . . ."[8]

A central metaphysical difference between the Sabbath and the rest of the week is that, on the Sabbath, the demonic is forbidden from going about its mischief. This freedom from the actions of the demonic brings about various changes in the liturgy and in the adept's behavior.[9] According to *Tiqqunei ha-Zohar* and *Ra'aya Meheimna,* this change in world-view creates the salient dynamic of the Sabbath mentality, *shinnui,* the changing of one's activity.

Tiqqunei ha-Zohar presents a lengthy homily on the Sabbath. This sermon combines pietistic exhortations with an esoteric doctrine of the Sabbath's inner nature:

> To observe the Sabbath, it must be changed from the days of the week, in one's clothing, food, and other delights. One who customarily eats two meals on the weekdays should eat three on the Sabbath, as it says: *Eat it today, for today is the Sabbath to God; you will not find it in the field* (Exodus 16:25). In all things, one should make an addition for the Sabbath. One who customarily has wine and bread on the weekdays should add meat as a Sabbath addition. *Change of action,* so that if one customarily behaves in a secular way, he should not do so on the Sabbath. . . . *Change of name,* for every day is called action, as it says: the *six days of action* (Ezekiel 46:1). But the seventh day is called the Sabbath, the negation of action. *Change of place,* that if one customarily lit a lamp on weekdays, he would change and not light it on the Sabbath, as it says: *Do not light fire in all your dwellings on the Sabbath day* (Exodus 35:3).[10]

Sabbath's dynamic of change has an underlying metaphysical rationale. On that day, the *Shekhinah* transforms from the elementary paradigm of the feminine to the transformative persona, the royal *Matronita*:

> One must change from the servant to the *Matronita,* that they not be equal. For the *Matronita* is the place of the Blessed Holy One. She must become royal, as it says: *She was there with her maidservants* (Esther 2:9) on the Sabbath. Moreover *in your dwellings*: a person's dwelling is his place. Also, *Change of place,* to prepare one's house for the Sabbath more than on the weekday. *Change of action,* that if he was sad on the weekday, let him rejoice on the Sabbath.[11]

Marital relationship is a metaphor for the doctrine of Divine union on the Sabbath. According to this well-known motif, sexual intercourse, on the Sabbath eve, evokes the union of the *Shekhinah* and *Tif'eret* that takes place in the cosmic realm:

> If a couple have had a dispute on the weekday, let them have peace on the Sabbath, that one not draw near to the elixir of death, the harlot, or to her husband, the pagan deity, the profanation of the Sabbath. So the sages taught: *If*

> *Israel would all keep one Shabbat according to the Law, they would be immediately redeemed.*[12] So one must change, with a lit candle, a made bed, and a set table. If he customarily lit a candle with one wick, let him add a second for the Sabbath. And if he customarily said the blessing for the bread over one loaf, let him add a second, like the second loaf [of the altar]. If he customarily argued with his wife on the weekdays, on the Sabbath let them have relations in peace. Therefore, the sexual duties of the sages are weekly, from Sabbath eve to Sabbath eve.[13]

The marital relationship is only a metaphor for the sage's primary relationship, which is with the *Shekhinah*: "One must differentiate the Sabbath from the week in all respects. If one is peaceful on all the days of the week, he should be all the more so on the Sabbath, conciliating her with great love, as it says with regard to the *Shekhinah*: *Open to me my sister, my bride, my dove, my innocent* (Song of Songs 5:2). With extra words of conciliation such as these a man placates his wife on the Sabbath."[14]

The changes that accompany the Sabbath reflect the travails of the Divine, the distension and exile that attend its emanation into the present world. A similar change is connected to the invocation of the Divine name. During prayer, that name is never pronounced audibly according the ineffable letters YHVH. The Divine name enters present reality only in secular fashion, with the euphemism *Adonay.* The separate essence of the name is comparable to the transformations of consciousness that accompany the Sabbath:

> Three upheavals: changing one's place, name, and action. Changing one's place, like the Blessed Holy One, of whom it says: *Behold, the Lord will go out of His place* (Isaiah 26:21). When the Lord comes out, He changes from judgment to mercy and from mercy to judgment so the Masters of the Mishnah taught: *Not as I am written am I said.*[15] In the world-to-come it will be written YHVH and pronounced YHVH. In this world, it is written YHVH and pronounced ADNY. This is change of place, for it is apart from its place that is the world-to-come. The world-to-come has no change, as it is written: *I am the Lord—I have not changed* (Malachi 3:6). It is

> written with the name YHVH and pronounced YHVH. This is called YHVH of Mercy, but apart from its place it changes and is called ADNY, Judgment. This is the secret meaning of standing up from the throne of Mercy and sitting on the throne of Judgment. . . . *Change of action* is the Sabbath, for all actions must be done with the back of the hand.[16] *Yad* [hand] is the *Ẓaddik*, *aḥar* (back) is the *Shekhinah*, and this is change of action.[17]

The dynamic of change is a metaphor for two states of the human condition: the exile and imprisonment of the soul in the corporeal body and the transformed essence of the Divine in the corporeal world. Change is also an underlying aspect of the scholar's exile and wandering:

> A man whom the Blessed Holy One has troubled with reincarnation, who has no success, let him be taken out of his place and put in another place, changing his place. This is the secret meaning of: *He will take other earth and plaster the house* (Leviticus 14:45), and this is change of place. When he sees that he is unsuccessful, *he will break down the house, its stones, and its beams* (ibid.). He is grafted into another body, as one might graft an apple tree onto a quince tree, changing the tree and its fruit; this is changing the name.[18]

The idealized and beatific nature of the Sabbath emphasizes only the benighted quality of the scholar's existence. According to the classical rabbinic and Zoharic teaching, the Sabbath is a context for the indwelling of the Divine. This indwelling of the Divine was also present in the *maskil*'s consciousness. The Sabbath comes to remedy the situation of the *maskil* by expediting this transformation of mentality.

The Sabbath Table

The Sabbath meal is a rite of great spiritual power in the Jewish tradition and was the focus of much interest in the theosophical Kabbalah. The meal is a ritual of unification, for the prayers and rites that attend the meal reflect the interaction of the *sefirot*, their ascent, descent, and union. These rituals, from the handwashing to the grace after the meals, unify the upper and lower *sefirot*.

Every halakhic aspect of the meal is invested with theurgic significance. Esoteric underpinnings for the various aspects of the meal include the breaking of the bread, handwashing, the "cup of blessing," Torah study at the meal, the inclusion of the poor at the table, the avoidance of gluttony, the second handwashing at the end of the meal, the benediction over a cup of wine, and the minimum amount for the cup and the meal.[19] The *Ra'aya Meheimna* and *Tiqqunim* develop the rabbinic motif of the Sabbath table as a paradigm of the Temple altar:[20]

> The cup has ten requirements,[21] as the Rabbis of the Mishnah taught, like the sum of *yud* from *yesod*, and they are crowning [in a beautiful cup], covering the table, immersion, rinsing, freshness, fullness, being taken with both hands, placed in the right, being contemplated and raised from the ground one handbreadth. These are a gift to all of the household. Crowning is from the crown of the holy covenant; covering like: *He wears light as a cloak* (Psalms 104:2), immersion and rinsing, immersion from without, rinsing from within, the secret meaning of: *They will be purified and made holy* (Leviticus 16:19).[22]

As the act of slaughter releases the animal for consumption, so the benedictions over the meal similarly release the food for consumption. Therefore, food eaten without a benediction is like meat unfit for consumption.[23]

The rabbinic dictum, *ba'al ha-bayit boẓe'a ve-oreaḥ mevarekh,* "The householder breaks the bread and the guest says the blessing,"[24] is interpreted in terms of the interaction of the *sefirot*. The householder represents the intermediate *sefirah Malkhut*, whereas the guest is the *sefirah Yesod*, which mediates union with the *Shekhinah*.

Besides the sexual union of the adept with his spouse, the interactions of society facilitate the Divine union on Friday night.[25] Inviting guests to the meal is an act of unification. Both actions reflect the sexual union of the *Shekhinah* with the Godhead:

> The Masters have taught: the breaker of bread is not allowed to eat until the members of the meal have answered *amen*, and they are not allowed to eat until he has. When the master of the house breaks the bread for those at the meal, not everyone has the same amount, for he need not divide equally. Sometimes he gives this one an olive-weight, or another an egg-weight. When they answer *amen* before the master of the house, they combine the two requisite amounts as one, an olive-weight or a egg-weight, that is YAHDVNHY.[26]

The motif of sexual union underlies the esoteric meaning of the two loaves of bread on the Sabbath table.[27] The term *boẓea* is a likely euphemism for the sexual act, whereas the bread itself also symbolizes the *Shekhinah*.[28] Even the crumbs are meaningful, as the minimum number of crumbs which make up the requirement of a blessing is ten, like the ten *sefirot*.[29] Hence, the meal is an act of unification of the *sefirot Tif'eret* and *Malkhut* through the medium of *Yesod*.

The equation of Sabbath hospitality with marital relations resolves the dilemma of those Sabbaths in which marital relations are impossible due to the interference of menstrual impurity. Hosting guests is a substitute act of unification, so that no Sabbath may pass without the mystic's commemorative act of unification.

In another exploration of the sexual metaphor, careless behavior at the Sabbath table is as heinous as sexual transgression:

> Whoever wastes morsels of bread, throwing them into an improper place, is like one who wastes the morsels of the brain, the drops of seed, throwing them upon the earth, of them it says: *For all flesh has corrupted its way upon the earth* (Genesis 6: 13). Such is the case whether he scattered them in a menstruous woman, a gentile, a maidservant, or a prostitute, and all the more so one who scatters the morsels of the bread of Torah, which are the jots and crowns . . . [30]

The sacraments of the altar and the Sabbath table are all performed with wine, because wine has two facets, white and red, representing the *sefirot Raḥamim* and *Din*.[31] This dual nature symbolizes the Sabbath mandates of remembrance and observance.[32] The wine is charged with metaphysical energies that themselves manipulate esoteric forces:

> *Wine will gladden a man's heart* (Psalms 104:15). This is the wine of Torah, as the coefficient (*gematria*) of "wine" (*yayin*) is "secret" (*sod*).[33] Just as wine has to be sealed and hidden, lest it be offered for idolatry, so the hidden secret Torah must be sealed, only drunk by those who are in awe of her. Hence there are many commandments regarding wine, for with it one blesses the Blessed Holy One. Wine has two colors, white and red, *Din* and *Raḥamim*, for its two aspects, like the crocus, white and red, white from the realm of the right, red from the realm of the left . . . [34]

As a result of this dual nature, wine may be employed for the demonic. *Yayin nesekh*, wine used for gentile sacraments, has taken on this demonic quality. Hence the stricture that the cup of sanctification must be rinsed and purified.[35] Rinsing the inside of the cup invokes the rabbinic trope *tokho ke-varo*, "consistent within and without," suggesting that the inner nature of the adept should be consistent with his comportment.[36]

The Two Domains

In *Tiqqunei ha-Zohar*, the Sabbath prohibition of carrying from *reshut ha-yaḥid* (a private domain) to *reshut ha-rabbim* (the public domain) is a metaphor for the defilement of the holy when it is brought into the realm of the demonic.[37] Rabbinic prohibitions against carrying items into or within the public domain guard against such metaphysical ruptures. God's private domain is the Sabbath, so that planting, uprooting, and carrying on that day are all aspects of the violation of the day's sacredness.[38] The secular banality that characterizes the public thoroughfare is also detrimental to the adept's practice. This is explained in this interpretation of the first statement of the Mishnah regarding the Sabbath:

> *Yeẓi'ot be-Shabbat shetayim*,[39] these are picking up and putting down in one action. One who takes something from its place

and leaves it elsewhere has uprooted the Tree of Life, the sign of the covenant, and placed it in a foreign domain. Whoever does this uproots a soul from one realm to another, that of the bile and the spleen. This causes the uprooting of Israel from the holy land to a foreign domain, *reshut ha-rabbim*,[40] as one who took his holy covenant into a foreign domain.[41]

The very term *rabbim* means, simultaneously, "the many" or "the public" and, in the spirit of the author's ongoing social critique, "the rabbis." The venture into the public thoroughfare is equated with entering the jurisdiction of the halakhic authorities.[42] Moreover, placing the covenant in a foreign domain is a reference to forbidden sexual relations, so that many forms of transgression are invoked in this image.

When the demonic is invoked, it is often in a welter of *kinnuyim* , as if opening the door to one image lets in a flood of attendant shades and demons. The demonic aspect of the public thoroughfare is characterized with many mythic images:

As much as one must guard the covenant, never taking it into a foreign domain[43] so one must guard the Sabbath, not taking [an object] from the private domain into the public domain. The private domain's width is four cubits, and they are YHVH, and its height is ten cubits and they are YU"D H"A VAV H"A. The public domain is the serpent, whore, elixir of a pagan deity, which is Samael. It is the essence of the seventy nations, the profaned harlot. Her mate is the profanation of the Sabbath. Therefore, one who takes from the private to the public domain is liable for stoning. The *'eruv* (Sabbath boundary) is the central pillar, in which one may carry from house to house, the higher and lower *Shekhinah* . . . [44]

The adept carries various apotropaic signs into the chaos of the public thoroughfare: the circumcision, *tefillin,* and the Sabbath itself. Notwithstanding these protections, leaving the inner precincts of the Sabbath for the demonic public thoroughfare has many risks:

The Sabbath is the sign of the covenant of circumcision, the sign of the *tefillin.* Whoever profanes one, it is as if he pro-

> fanes the other. The *tefillin* of the head are for *Remember* [the Sabbath day] and the *tefillin* of the hand are for *Observe* [the Sabbath day]. As the public thoroughfare is the desecration of the Sabbath, so the sign of the covenant has the prostitute as its desecration, the foreign thoroughfare.[45]

The public thoroughfare has a quality of sexual illicitness[46] and is equated, perhaps realistically, with the prostitute, in this case the debased and demonic aspect of the *Shekhinah*.[47] Masturbation and coitus interruptus profane the holy by casting seed into the demonic realm.[48] Thus, the theme of the two *reshuyot* is often accompanied by the motif of illicit sexuality: "Whoever carries out of the private domain and into the public domain, or spills seed from the sign of the holy covenant bringing it to a foreign domain, has planted the Tree of Knowledge of Good and Evil. Hence, it says of whoever implants a prostitute, a maidservant, a gentile woman or a menstruous woman: *You shall make no idol* (Exodus 20:4)."[49]

Profaning God's name is also a violation of boundaries. The Divine name originates in the transcendent and abstracted upper *sefirot*. Profanation brings it stillborn into the falsehood and artifice of present reality. In the same way, the *'eruv*, or Sabbath boundary, creates a sanctified realm of sacred symbols. In the exile, observance of the Sabbath requires withdrawal into such a closed sanctuary, free from the corruptions of secular influence. Defilement of the Sabbath is comparable to the fall, in that each catastrophe is allegorized as blasphemy and idolatry.[50]

The private domain, *reshut ha-yaḥid*, is the sacred realm. The *'eruv*, the boundary that creates this domain, is the unifying *sefirah Tif'eret*. The rabbinic dimensions of the private domain, four cubits and ten handbreadths, represent the four letters YHVH and the ten *sefirot*.[51] The various boundaries also have different meanings. The *'eruv* encompasses all of the upper *sefirot*, whereas the *mavoi* or blind alley includes the lower *Shekhinah*. These boundaries are represented in the shapes of Hebrew letters: "An *'eruv*, in which one lowers the beam when it exceeds twenty handbreadths,[52] is the *Yu"d* above the *Ka"f* of *Keter*. Therefore, a blind alley, the lower *Shekhinah*, measures of ten handbreadths. One must lower the beam that is the letter *vav.*"[53]

All of these understandings originate in the experience of Sabbath activity. The private, encircled areas, *reshut ha-yaḥid,* are the sanctified realm. Otherwise, the practitioner is adrift in *reshut ha-rabbim.* The prohibition of carrying and picking things up bars the adept from interaction with his environment, which evokes the shifting, alienated nature of the exile. The Sabbath observer passes, wraithlike, through the corporeal domain. This alienation from present reality is the didactic goal of the mystic's experience of *reshut ha-rabbim.* Observance of the Sabbath is a withdrawal into the realm of the sacred. Rather than being a celebration of the wonder of the created world, the holy day is a sanctuary, a refuge from the profane realities of existence.

Prayer as Unification

In the theosophical Kabbalah, prayer has a soteric function as a vehicle of transformation. Prayer redeems the practitioner at the level of *Malkhut.*[54] Petitional prayer is, therefore, a act of mystical ascent and quest: "Like the stone flung by a sling, one must direct one's prayer to a known place. One must fling one's thought in prayer to that Crown that is encrusted with gems, of which is says: *When bowing, bow at Barukh and straighten at the name,* with the name toward which one needs to send it."[55]

The recitation of psalms, when coupled with the act of repentance, takes the place of penitential sacrifice.[56] Even the daily petitional prayers are part of this process. In fact, they are its center, for the very nature of blessing is an invocation of the upper *sefirot*: "BaRUKH (blessed) is KH'—*Keter,* R'—*Reshit*[57] *Ḥokhmah* B' the transcendent Mother and the *Shekhinah* U' [58] for the six *sefirot,* even ten are included in it and gathered in."[59]

The *Tiqqunim* interpreted two rabbinic dicta in terms of the theurgic act of unifying the upper and lower *sefirot.* The talmudic dictum *kore'a be-varukh, zoqef ba-shem,* or "bow at the blessing, straighten at the Name,"[60] refers to the proper bows to be taken during the recitation of the daily prayer. The adherent bows at the word *Barukh,* literally, "Blessed," and straightens up at the recitation of the name of God. *Tiqqunei ha-Zohar* stresses the theurgic aspects of bowing and straightening, to indicate the approach, coupling, and union of the upper and lower worlds.

The bow directs the descent of the higher aggregate aspects of the Divine to unification with the lower. The effect is intensified through the release of serpentine energies in the spine, as indicated by the rabbinic admonition that one must continue praying "even if a serpent is coiled at one's heel."[61] The act blends the powers of the name *YHVH*, the energies of the *sefirah Tif'eret*, with the powers of the audible manifestation of the name *Adonai*. This action brings the union of *Tif'eret* with *Malkhut*: "When he bows, all the cherubs shelter him with their wings, which is the *sekhakh* [thatch] of the Sukkah. *Zoqef*—he straightens with the two names *AHYH* and *YHVH*."[62]

The bows of the petitional prayer are true theurgy, in that they invoke the immanent presence of God. The union of these realms is also symbolized in the motif of the matriarch Rebekah's leaning down to empty her water jug, the Hebrew *kad*. The numerical coefficient of *kad* is twenty-four, also the number of books in the Bible, implying that Scripture is also a conduit of this immanent Divinity.[63] The act of prayer, like the mystical exegesis of Scripture, is an act that brings about unification: "The twenty-four letters [of the second line of the *shema* prayer] include the twenty-four books, the *kad* withdraws from the sea of Torah. . . . What does this *kad* draw forth? The *Shekhinah*, which is the twenty-four books of the Torah."[64]

The prostrations also invoke the dimensional nature of the six intermediate *sefirot*. They are compared to shaking the *lulav*, another theurgic act that invokes the flow of the ineffable Divine into corporeal existence: "These bendings and straightenings demonstrate the principle of back and forth, for He that owns the four winds; up and down for He that owns the heaven and the earth.[65] These are the six dimensions: heaven and earth and the four directions . . . "[66]

This action also invokes the people Israel's role as the support for the vicissitudes of the *Shekhinah* in her exile. The proper intention or understanding at times of prayer affects the *Shekhinah*'s condition: "Happy are you, Israel, the feet of the

Shekhinah, when you stand on them in the *Amidah* prayer, truly standing on them, standing on them in the exile, when YHVH descends on you, as it says: *When you straighten, straighten at the Name,* for a person must straighten and rise to the *Shekhinah.*"[67]

Straightening invokes the union of the *sefirot Malkhut* and *Tif'eret,* which is indicated in the combined name *YAHDVNHY.* This combinations of the names *YHVH* and *ADNY* came to be a standard usage in kabbalistic liturgy. In sefirotic terms, the linking of *Tif'eret* and *Malkhut* through *Yesod* channels Divine effluence into the corporeal and returns Divine thought to the ineffable.[68] Not surprisingly, this practice is repeated ten times[69] in the prayer service.

The rabbinic dicta *ha-roẓeh le-haḥkim yadrim,* "he who desires wisdom should (turn) south," and *ha-roẓeh le-ha'ashir yaẓpin,* "he who desires wealth should turn north,"[70] refer prayer toward different areas in the Temple court. It originated, historically, at the point of transition between cultic sacrifice and personal prayer. Its original application seems to have been as a theurgic addendum to the Temple cult, as the altar's table was located in the north side of the sacrificial area.

These dicta went to the heart of a theological problem that preoccupied kabbalistic speculation. The shifting exchanges of energy in the ten *sefirot* tempted the practitioners to devise prayers that would address specific *sefirot.* The kabbalists were concered with whether the adherent could direct prayer toward one *sefirah* or another. Potentially, this practice was heretical in that it implied divisions in the absolute unity of the *sefirot.* Because the *sefirot* were meant to be in union, to visualize a separation in the Divine was gnostic heresy. This direction of energies toward various aspects of the sacrificial cult provides an important precedent for the direction of intention towards specific *sefirot*:

> One might ask: Why do we pray to the Blessed Holy One on several levels? Sometimes one prays through a certain *sefirah* or attribute, sometimes one's prayer is to the right, as it says; *ha roẓeh le-haḥkim yadrim,* sometimes to the left, which is sig-

> nified by *ha roẓeh le-ha'ashir yaẓpin.* Sometimes to the central pillar, sometimes to the *ẓaddik.* Every prayer goes up to a certain level, but YHVH is truly in every *sefirah.*[71]

The practicing kabbalist confronted a dilemma. On the one hand, he might perceive that cosmic or social orders were beset by an imbalance in the energies of the *sefirot.* Due to its theurgic power, his properly directed mystical prayer could correct that imbalance. Yet at the same time, the kabbalist could not direct prayer only toward the *sefirah* in question. Full intention, during prayer, to a particular *sefirah* is equivalent to the gnostic heresy of *kiẓẓuẓ ba-neti'ot,* "cutting the shoots," the imaging of divisions, as opposed to unity, in the Divine.[72] Such directed prayer, then, could emphasize a certain realm, predicated on the understanding that the *sefirot* as a whole were unified. This directing of prayer is an act of balancing and compensation. In the present case, the direction of prayer does not originate from an ongoing bias on the part of the adherent; there are merely different needs for the *Shekhinah* at different times: "Prayer is the *Shekhinah.* When one asks mercy on the world, she goes on the right, when she has to bring judgment on the world she goes to the left, and all of these are for YHVH who is everywhere . . . "[73]

This paradox of unity and multiplicity makes use of the classical Zoharic preoccupation with the four rivers that flowed out from the Garden of Eden. Just as these rivers all derived from a single source, so the mystic's directed prayers are absorbed by the unified network of the *sefirot*: "*A river issues from Eden to water the garden and it then divides and becomes four branches* (Genesis 2:10) that is *Ḥesed,* the right arm. Then *he who desires wisdom, let him turn south.* The camp of Michael drink from it, with Judah's staff and two tribes. *Gevurah* is the left arm, so *he who desires wealth, let him turn north,* the camp of Gavriel drink from it, with the staff of Dan and two tribes . . . "[74]

This statement compares the multiplicity of the *sefirot,* which make up the unity of God, with the multiplicity of the tribes and the heavenly host, which also make up the unity of Israel and the cosmos. Kabbalah also contains principles of balancing and compensation in which the *sefirot* originate in their opposites. For instance, there is the paradox of the dynamic, extroverted *sefirah Ḥesed* originating in the ineffability of the *sefirah Ḥokhmah.*[75]

These rabbinic dicta regarding prayer are interpreted by the author of the *Tiqqunim in* terms of the interaction of the *sefirot*. In each case, the rabbinic dictum is reduced to the *kinnui* form, then reinterpreted symbolically. In the case of the bowings and straightenings, this sefirotic interpretation is original and novel. The dictum concerning directed prayer towards areas of the Temple has a more direct link to the motif of *sefirot* as aspects of the Divine. The theme of prayer as theurgic intercession would remain in subsequent Kabbalah and acquire great resonance during the Safed revival.

Conclusions

Generally, a work that continues a tradition set by a larger, prior work might be considered as the less significant of the two. Critical scholarship generally deprecates the importance of the secondary text. It has been the position of this study that such is not the case with the works of the author of *Tiqqunei ha-Zohar* and *Ra'aya Meheimna.* Even though the *Tiqqunim* are, by their own definition, secondary to the Zohar, they develop the Zohar's mystical world-view in ways that are significant for subsequent Kabbalah. The Zohar is the central work of theosophical Kabbalah but the *Tiqqunim* and *Ra'aya Meheimna* are instrumental in creating a context for the acceptance of the Zohar and the subsequent historical developments of movements of kabbalistic thought.

The vocation of the *maskil,* which *Tiqqunei ha-Zohar* and *Ra'aya Meheimna* formalized, demanded that the adept emulate the Zohar's contemplative spirituality, particularly the romantic ethic of picaresque religious quest as practiced by Rabbi Shimon Bar Yoḥai and his disciples. The anonymous kabbalist who wrote *Tiqqunei ha-Zohar* and *Ra'aya Meheimna* defined this social ethic so that this purportedly Tannaitic life-style could be carried into his contemporary milieu. According to this doctrine of religious vocation, mystical enlightenment came from the practice of contemplative Torah study, utilizing the symbolic hermeneutic that had been crystalizing among the theosophical kabbalists. This pietism was not only contemplative; the mystic was socially activist in his struggle to achieve the Zohar's theurgic goals.[1]

It is the position of this study that *Tiqqunei ha-Zohar* and *Ra'aya Meheimna* also had an important role in the development of kabbalistic hermeneutics. The author 's doctrinal additions to the Zohar's theosophical Kabbalah were critical in shaping the perception of the Zohar by later kabbalists. Subsequent interpretations of the Zohar were also influenced by his doctrinal innovations, which include his understandings of the immanence of God, the emanating structure of the successive worlds and the relation of Divinity to the kabbalistic symbol, or *kinnui.* His tendency to "read" those doctrines, as well as the conclusions of the *Idrot,* into preexistent Zoharic texts prefigured the methodology of later exegeses in the Cordovero and Lurianic schools of thought. Every subsequent school, in interpreting the Zohar, was bound to accept the the author's doctrinal innovations and to find them in the earlier strata of the Zohar, just as the *Tiqqunim* and *Ra'aya Meheimna* did.

The quality of urgency in Jewish history was dramatized in these works' portrayal of the legendary catastrophes of the Pentateuch as continuing to unfold in contemporary history. In this drama of unfolding catastrophe and mythic chaos, the *maskil* is portrayed as struggling to find meaning for the dilemmas of humanity. It is not the purpose of this study to trace the resonance of this imagery in subsequent kabbalistic movements. However, it may be assumed that the images of struggle, brokenness, and distension emphasized in Lurianic Kabbalah, with such effect in Jewish history, have their seed in the *Tiqqunim* and *Ra'aya Meheimna.*

The heightened social and soteric roles of the enlightened mystic are portrayed as a fitting continuation of the heroic legend of Shimon Bar Yoḥai and his circle. Hence, there is a historical connection between the romanticism of the Zohar, the *Tiqqunim,* and *Ra'aya Meheimna* and the the spiritual movements of Safed, Sabbateanism, and Polish Ḥasidism. These later movements sought to continue the spiritual model of the heroic mystic, whose example and actions are as significant as his teachings. It is the conclusion of this study that the teachings of the *Tiqqunim* and *Ra'aya Meheimna* self-consciously attempted to expedite this historical process. Therefore, they serve as an important bridge between the Zohar and the development of subsequent kabbalistic movements.

Because the *Tiqqunim* and *Ra'aya Meheimna* came to have such an important historical role, the author's relationship to *halakhah* requires clarification. Jewish mysticism, in general, developed from the pre-existent, highly contextualized ontology of rabbinic Judaism. Jewish tradition shaped this kabbalist's expectations; its theological aims limited the parameters of his experiences. The author's use of rabbinic texts as kabbalistic symbols, or *kinnuyim,* belies the accusation that his attitude towards the *halakhah* was antinomian. His utilization of rabbinic materials in the *kinnui* form, combined with his understanding of the immanent function of the Divine in the chaos of contemporary history, demonstrate that the law and lore of the Talmud are intrinsic to present existence and redemption from its dilemmas.

The author's understanding of the ritual and civil laws of Judaism do contain a number of important departures from their nature of biblical and rabbinic origins. *Tiqqunei ha-Zohar* and *Ra'aya Meheimna* utilize the nuances of the dietary and ritual traditions to reinforce the performance of the *miẓvah* as a charged act that directly causes change and repair in the Divine macrocosm. Such an understanding of the *miẓvot* certainly preceded these works in the traditions of the theosophical Kabbalah.[2] Nonetheless, *Tiqqunei ha-Zohar* and *Ra'aya Meheimna* judiciously use halakhic material, particularly in their exploration of the mnemonics and repeated principles that so animate talmudic debate. It is true that the *Tiqqunim* and *Ra'aya Meheimna* contain proportionately more rabbinically based arguments, and that those arguments draw on a deeper and more theoretical level of halakhic thought than the other parts of the Zohar. This charged use of *halakhah* was particularly effective when combined with the anthropomorphic conclusions of the *Idrot*.

The practices presented in this study are not specific to the *maskil*; all were basic acts of piety incumbent upon the entire community. The *maskil* only brings a greater degree of consciousness to the action. Inevitably, then, the *maskil* is fated to lead, as he alone knows the inner meaning of the popular practice. Only the *maskil* understands the ontological state of the world, particularly the chaotic nature of existence. He is the one most conscious of this level of reality; hence he perceives most clearly the demonic nature of those entities that the law considers unclean, unfit, and forbidden. Certainly, the outline of these proscriptions are the contours of the demonic's empirical existence. Consequently, the *maskil* also understands best the theurgic dimension of the *miẓvot*.

Preoccupation with the exoteric dimension of the law is seduction into apostasy, for legal casuistries that refine the laws may stray into a voided realm of religious sophistry. So it is that the vocation of the *maskil* at times overlaps with that of the legalist, but the former is not in full agreement with the latter. There is an essential level of *halakhah*, in which the legalist and mystic are united by shared purpose. The halakhists' flaw lies in their application of a voided, sophistic casuistry to the essence of the *halakhah*. This mentality also lent itself to the nihilism of rationalistic philosophy, which was itself the object of numerous polemics in the Zohar and works of Moshe de Leon.

In the light of this extensive use of the tropes of the law in the *Tiqqunim* and *Ra'aya Meheimna*, it is clear that the author distinguishes between the primary binding nature of the commandments themselves and the potentially flawed purview of the rabbinical authorities, who he freely criticizes. The author also makes a distinction between *halakhah* as part of the symbolic canon, in which its deeper meaning is implied by aspects of its surface nature, and the empty casuistry of many contemporary rabbis. There is an inherent skepticism about this human authority, yet a reverence for the essential identity of the Torah and its laws. In this regard, the doctrines of the Torah of

Aẓilut and Torah of *Beriah* represent gradations and dimensions of the same Torah, even as the worlds of *Aẓilut* and *Beriah* describe dimensions of the same whole macrocosmos.

This understanding of the law's transcendent aspect is also part of the *maskil's* enlightenment. The same heightened consciousness that understands the inner meaning of the sacred text perceives the esoteric dimension of the laws and practices. This is particularly true when the *maskil* has been initiated into the innermost dimension of the law, the anthropomorphic mysteries of the *Idrot*. These traditions provide the *maskil* with a window into his own soul, through which he gains an understanding of the innermost nature of existence. This understanding creates an almost yogic awareness of the movements of forces across the human body and the Divine macrocosm.

The mysterious figure who wrote *Tiqqunei ha-Zohar* and *Ra'aya Meheimna* was truly the principal acolyte of the Zohar. By accepting the Zohar as an entity and internalizing it, he created the ethic of subsequent Kabbalah in its most popular, widespread, and historically significant incarnations. Moreover, *Tiqqunei ha-Zohar* and *Ra'aya Meheimna* may be read in such a way as to portray a unified view of this mystic's dark and beautiful inner world.

Notes

Chapter One Notes

1. *Or Yaqar-Tiqqunei ha-Zohar I,* 1:3 (c. 1550).

2. See Gershom Scholem, "The Meaning of the Torah in Jewish Mysticism," *On the Kabbalah and Its Symbolism* (New York: Schocken Books, 1965).

3. See Gershom Scholem, *Major Trends in Jewish Mysticism,* 3rd ed. (New York: Schocken Books, 1961), pp. 159–163; *Kabbalah* (New York: Meridian Books, 1978), pp. 214–219; Isaiah Tishby and Fischel Lachover, *Mishnat ha-Zohar* I (henceforth *MhZ*), 2 vol. (Jerusalem: Mossad Bialik, 1971), pp. 25–28; Elliot Wolfson, Introduction to *Sefer ha-Rimmon* (Atlanta: Scholars Press, 1988), pp. 3–9; Yehudah Liebes, "Ha-Mitos ha-Kabbali she-be-fi Orfeos" [The Kabbalistic Mythos in the Teaching of Orpheus], *Jerusalem Studies in Jewish Thought* 7; no. 1 (1988): 432n. Liebes has most recently extended the research into the Zohar's origins, particularly the variant texts of the *Idrot,* in his essay "Keiẓad Nitḥabber Sefer ha-Zohar?" [How Was the Zohar Composed?], in *The Zohar and it's Generation,* Jerusalem Studies in Jewish Thought 8, ed. Joseph Dan (Jerusalem: Magnes Press, 1989), pp. 1–71.

4. The inner nature of the *Idrot* and their relationship to the Zohar has been examined by Yehudah Liebes in "Keiẓad Nitḥabber Sefger ha-Zohar?" and "Ha-Mashiaḥ shel ha-Zohar" [The Messiah of the Zohar], in *Ha-Ra'ayon ha-Meshiḥi be-Yisrael* (Jerusalem: Magnes Press, 1982), pp. 87–236. Liebes has also speculated on the nature of

the circles that produced the Zohar and their influence on Moshe de Leon. This is a necessary development in kabbalah studies and should provide for a less charged and doctrinal understanding of the Zohar's origins.

5. The presence of a characteristic single hand was acknowledged by R. Avraham Galante, in the great anthology of Zohar commentaries, *Or ha-Ḥamah I* (c. 1550) 159a: "these are the words of the book's author in the days of the *Geonim,* or other sages who gathered the articles of R. Abba, R. Shimon Bar Yoḥai's scribe, and divided them according to the readings of the year . . . "

6. *Tiqqun* is one of the Zohar's euphemisms for the *sefirot,* or Divine hypostases, which are the central organizing principle of classical Kabbalah. The *Tiqqunim,* in particular, employ this term as an organizing principle of the text's literary form. The term derives from the Arabic اتقن, to complete, render firm, construct well" (Lane, *An Arabic-English Lexicon* I:I, p. 309), "finir, se rendre raison de . . .," (R. Dozy, *Supplement aux Dictionaries Arabes,* p. 149).

7. The idea of seventy faces or aspects to the Torah is a classical rabbinic formulation. See Moshe Idel, "Infinities of Torah in Kabbalah," in *Midrash and Literature,* ed. Geoffrey H. Hartman and Sanford Budick, (New Haven, Conn.: Yale University Press, 1986), p. 155n.

8. A large section from the *Tiqqun* 70 is included in the main part of the Zohar, I 22a–29a. R. Moshe Cordovero, in his commentary *Or Yaqar* (c. 1567) also indicates that the lengthy selection *Ta Ḥazei* (TZḤ 7b, Z I 256a–262a) is also "from the *Tiqqunim*" (*Or Yaqar* III; p. 277). The author of the *Tiqqinum* also wrote the preface to the romantic composition *Saba de-Mishpatim* (Z II 94a–b) according to Tishby, *MhZ* I, p. 19n. See also Yehudah Liebes's *Peraqim be-Millon Sefer ha-Zohar* [Some Chapters in a Zohar Lexicon] (Ph.D. dissertation, Hebrew University, 1976; Jerusalem: Hebrew University Press, 1982) p. 322. The gloss of the Zohar's treatise on physiognomy, *Raza de-Razin* (II 70a–75a, ZḤ 56c–60a) in *Zohar Ḥadash* 31a–35b, seems to be by the author of the *Tiqqunim.*

A composition included in *Sefer ha-Malkhut* (Paris #841), an anthology of the writings of Joseph of Hamadan, was identified by the late Ephraim Gottlieb as coming from the same hand as *Tiqqunei ha-Zohar* and *Ra'aya Meheimna* ("Shenei Ḥibburim Nosafim le-Rav Yosef ha-Ba mi-Shushan ha-Birah ve-Zihui ha-Ḥibburim she-be-'Sefer ha-Malkut' " [Two Additional Compositions by R. Joseph of Shushan and the Identification of the Compositions in *Sefer ha-Malkhut*], in

Meḥqarim be-Sifrut ha-Kabbalah [Studies in Kabbalistic Literature], ed. Joseph Hacker). Gottlieb compiled a number of the author's unpublished Hebrew writings. Amos Goldreich of Tel Aviv University has edited a number of these manuscripts, and we hope they will be published imminently. At this time one has been made available, in the essay "La'az Iberi be-Fragment Bilti-Yadu'a shel Ba'al Tiqqunei ha-Zohar" [Iberian Dialect in an Unknown Fragment from the Author of Tiqqunei ha-Zohar], in *The Zohar and Its Generation,* pp. 89–121.

9. The extant manuscripts of *Tiqqunei ha-Zohar* may be divided into four "families." The first and largest resembles the printed editions of the *Tiqqunim* and generally begin at TZ 17a, with the "second introduction," the famous preamble by Elijah the Prophet, "Pataḥ Eliyahu." Within this family are a number of smaller groupings. Some texts omit the first *Tiqqun* of the Mantua and Orta Koj editions, thereby altering the numbering of all the subsequent *Tiqqunim* (Cambridge ADD 519, ADD 1833; J.T.S. 1644). Other texts truncate the third *Tiqqun* (British Museum REG 16A XIV 765 and OR 10701 GS 1398), and still other texts omit *Tiqqun* 13 (British Museum ADD 27061 782). Some texts append material from Tiqqunei Zohar Hadash to the end (Sasson 591, Vatican 200). This Introduction from the printed edition rarely appears (Mousaioff 218, Cambridge ADD 519), although material from it may be scattered throughout the text (Vienna-Reiner 218). This would support the idea that, as in the Mantua edition of the Zohar, the introduction is an artificial construct included after the assembly of the main material (this is supported by the inclusion of material from the introduction in the *Tiqqunei Zohar Hadash* of Cordovero's *Or Yaqar*). Such is also the case with material from the lengthy *Tiqqunim* 21, 69, and 70, which are shorter in many manuscripts in this family. The material in Zohar I, 22a–22a, appears in certain manuscripts in this family, though not always in the same place (Vatican 208, Paris 791).

A second family of manuscripts are those texts presently included in *Tiqqunei Zohar Ḥadash.* These may be presented in a manner similar to its published form (Oxford M337–1917, Sasson 27) or according to the format of Cordovero's *Or Yaqar.* This latter group is particularly important because the texts are very exact yet lacking in many embellishments and interpolations found in the Orts Koj text, to which material has been added. The British Museum manuscript of *Or Yaqar* (ADD 37060-781, ADD 27061-782, ADD 27063-783 and particularly ADD 27041-784 and ADD 27042-785) contain Zohar texts not otherwise found in the printed edition.

A third family of manuscripts is exemplified by Vatican 207 (1489) and British Museum OR 10863-GS 1097. This family seems to bear no resemblance to the structure of the printed edition and makes extensive use of the marginal material included in *Tiqqunim* 21, 69, and 70. Sometimes the copyist seems to have randomly combined disparate sections, often switching section in midsentence, as if he did not understand what he was writing. At the same time, there is much substitution of Hebrew for Aramaic and other paraphrasing.

The fourth family of manuscripts is exemplified by Paris 791. Its most salient feature is that the extra *Tiqqunim* of TZ 139a–148a are inserted into the text in the vicinity of TZ 38b. This text, or one like it, was used extensively by Reuven Margoliot in the preparation of his edition of the *Tiqqunim* and is responsible for much of the difference between that edition and the standard Orta Koj edition.

The Zohar project of the Hebrew University, under the directorship of the late Rivka Shatz, collected some fifty-five manuscripts that were initially listed as *Tiqqunei ha-Zohar.* Of these, some are really texts of the *Idra Rabbah,* mislabeled (Firenza 53, J.T.S. 2203, Vatican 226). Other manuscripts contain "Tiqqunim", that is, Lurianic devotional practices, but they are also not *Tiqqunei ha-Zohar* (J.T.S. 1582, 1584, 1650; British Museum OR 10385-GS 238).

10. For example, *Tiqqunim* 10 and 21 deal largely with the issue of prayer, whereas *Tiqqun* 67 deals with the sin of Adam. In the lengthy *Tiqqunim* 69 and 70, the author extends his excurses into later sections of the book of Genesis. *Tiqqun* 21 (TZ 42b–63a) portrays a somewhat more elaborate setting of the heavenly academy and has a more developed structure than the other *Tiqqunim.*

11. Scholem, *Major Trends,* p. 157.

12. See Elliot Wolfson, Introduction to *Sefer ha-Rimmon,* Chapter 4.

13. In the published editions, the text of the *Ra'aya Meheimna* was broken up and incorporated into the main sections of the Zohar, with each extant commandment placed according to the Torah portion in which it appears. In the Cremona and Mantua editions of the Zohar, the text of the *Ra'aya Meheimna* was confused with another treatise on commandments, *Piqqudim,* which seems to have been composed by Moshe de Leon.

It is possible to reconstruct the structure of the *Ra'aya Meheimna* with the help of the numbering system of R. Moshe Zakhut (known by his acronym as the *ReMeZ*) and the studies of E. Gottlieb, "Ma'amarei ha-'Piqqudim' she-be-Zohar" [The "Commandments" Passages in the Zohar] in *Meḥqarim be-Sifrut ha-Kabbalah,* pp.224–229. Cordovero's *Or Yaqar* separates the two treatises, and Cordovero acknowledged their distinction in his *Or Ne'erav* (3:3, 4:2). The manuscript of *Or Yaqar* contains observations about the identity of various Zoharic texts. The Cordovero version of *Ra'aya Meheimna* has recently been published as part of the *Or Yaqar* commentary.

It is regrettable that Reuven Margoliot chose to accept the unity of the two compositions with faith in its Tannaitic origins, in his *Ra'aya Meheimna, Sefer Miẓvot* [. . . A Book of the Commandments, in the first volume of his edition of the Zohar], after the manner of R. David Luria in his *Kadmut Sefer ha-Zohar* [The Antiquity of the Zohar] (New York: Nezaḥ, 1951).

The following seem to be the extant texts of the *Ra'aya Meheimna:*

I: 252a, 246b, 226a–b

II: 41b–43a, 93a, 114a–121a, 157b.

III: 3b, 16b, 20a, 24b, 27a–29b, 33a, 34a, 42a, 67b, 81b–83b, 89b–90a, 98a–b, 108b–110b, 111a, 121a–126a, 152b–153b, 175a, 215a–217a, 217b–220a, 222a–239a, 242a–258a, 271b, 274a, 274b–283a.

Breaking up the main text of the *Ra'aya Meheimna* did have a negative effect on the coherency of the text, as R. Avraham Galante (*Or ha-Ḥamah II,* p. 148b) noted: "The publishers broke up these commandments and wrote each one in its own place, and their destruction was greater than their building, for the understanding of many issues is contingent on the commandment which precedes them, and this disruption leaves things obscure and out of context."

14. TZ 136a.

15. RM III 223b.

16. RM II 114b.

17. Amos Goldreich ("La'az Iberi be-fragment Bilti-Yadu'a shel Ba'al *Tiqqunei ha-Zohar,*" pp. 91n, 96n) lists a number of datings of the *Tiqqunim,* citing Scholem (*Major Trends,* p. 188; and *Kabbalah,* p. 59) as placing the text in the late thirteenth or early fourteenth century. Tishby (MhZ II, p. 393n) and Scholem (*Kabbalah,* p. 232) had also dated the works prior to 1312, that being the target year of various eschatological predictions that they make.

18. TZḤ, 103b, 115a; TZ, 111z, 115a.

19. RM III 82a, 257a.

20. TZ 96a, possibly TZ 132b.

21. RM III 282a, TZ 7a; see also Scholem, *Kabbalah* p. 228. Amos Goldreich has traced the use of this term into Portugal and North Africa, thus qualifying the Castilean origin of the *Tiqqunim* ("La'az Iberi be-Fragment Bilti-Yadu'a sehl Ba'al *Tiqqunei ha-Zohar,*" pp. 91–93).

22. TZ 96a.

23. TZ 70b.

Chapter Two Notes

1. One might say that the *Tiqqunim* are a late strand of the Jewish canon. The address of the prophet Elijah, *Pataḥ Eliyahu,* which makes up the second introduction to the main text of the *Tiqqunim* (TZ 17a–b), was incorporated into the daily and pre-Sabbath rite of the Lurianic liturgy. The meditation on the *shofar* (RM III 98b) is also commonly printed in the Rosh ha-Shanah service of the Sefardic and Ḥassidic communities. If a work is incorporated into the liturgy, its mere recitation, even without comprehension, is still perceived as having a positive effect. If this liturgical application is equal to Jewish canonicity, then the *Tiqqunim* themselves are canonical.

2. See Gershom Scholem, *Origins of the Kabbalah* (Princeton, N.J.: Jewish Publication Society and Princeton University Press, 1987), pp. 35–48.

3. The spirituality of theosophical Kabbalah is particularly evident in the works of Isaac the Blind, Ezra and Azriel of Gerona, Naḥmanides, Moses de Burgos, Todros Abulafia, the brothers Jacob and Isaac ben Jacob ha-Cohen de Soria, Isaac ben Samuel of Acre, Jacob Ben Sheshet, Joseph Ben Scholem Ashkenazi, Joseph Gikatilla, Shem Tov Ibn Gaon, and the works of Moshe de Leon.

4. The use of symbols in Kabbalah is addressed in Joseph Dan, "Midrash and the Dawn of Kabbalah" in Geoffrey H. Hartman and Sanford Budick, eds., *Midrash and Literature* (New Haven, Conn.: Yale University Press, 1986), pp. 127–139; Moshe Idel, *Kabbalah: New Perspectives* (New Haven, Conn.: Yale University Press, 1988) pp. 173–249; "Infinities of Torah in Kabbalah" in *Midrash and Literature,* pp. 141–157; Gershom Scholem, "The Meaning of the Torah in Jewish Mysticism," in *On the Kabbalah and Its Symbolism,* pp. 32–86, "The Name of God and Linguistic Theory of the Kaballah," *Diogenes, no.* 79–80 (1972): pp. 59–80, 164–94; Isaiah Tishby, "Ha-Semel ve-ha-Dat ba-Kabbalah" [Symbol and Religion in Kabbalah], in *Netivei Emunah u-Minut* [Paths of Faith and Heresy] (Jerusalem: Magnes Press, 1982), pp. 11–22. See also Elliot Wolfson, "By Way of Truth: Aspects

of Naḥmanides' Kabbalistic Hermeneutic," *AJS Review* 14; no. 2 (1989): 116–117, note 43.

5. See *Bereshit Rabbah* 1:4.

6. Elliot Wolfson ("The Hermeneutics of Visionary Experience: Revelation and Interpretation in the Zohar," *Religion* 18 [1988]: 311–345) has demonstrated that the hermeneutic experience of symbolic reading is equated by the Zohar with prophetic vision itself. Hence, a great crisis of post-exilic Judaism, the cessation of prophecy, was also resolved through the elevation of this hermeneutic experience.

7. Cf. Frank Talmage, "Apples of Gold: The Inner Meaning of Sacred Texts in Medieval Judaism," p. 329; in *Jewish Spirituality I,* ed. Art Green (New York: Crossroad, 1986): "Each *sefirah* in the kabbalistic systems of exegesis is assigned one or more divine names as well as a plethora of epithets and cognomens which make the biblical text a network of allusions to what transpires in the world of the *sefirot,* to be deciphered by those who know the code."

8. Z I 262b, II 15b, 140b; TZ 36a, 71b; Tishby, MhZ *I* pp. 298–301. See Alexander Altmann, *Essays in Jewish Intellectual History* (Hanover, N.H.: University Press of New England, 1981), pp. 161–179; Joseph Dan, *Torat ha-Sod shel Ḥasidei Ashkenaz* [The Esoteric Traditions of the German Ḥasidim] (Jerusalem: Bialik, 1968), pp. 207–10, 257–58; Yehudah Liebes, *Peraqim be-Millon Sefer ha-Zohar,* p. 25; Scholem, *On the Kabbalah and Its Symbolism,* p. 54; Elliot Wolfson, "Circumcision and the Divine Name: A Study in the Transmission of an Esoteric Doctrine," *Jewish Quarterly Review* 78 nos. 1–2 (1987): pp. 93–94.

9. See Frank Talmage, "Apples of Gold" pp. 321–325.

10. TZ 24b; RM III 3b, 244a. See also Arthur Green, "The Song of Songs in Early Jewish Mysticism," ORIM 2, no. 2: 49–63; Ira Chernus, *Mysticism in Rabbinic Judaism* (Berlin: Walter de Gruyter, 1983), p. 27; Saul Lieberman, "Mishnat Shir ha-Shirim" in Gershom Scholem, *Jewish Gnosticism, Merkabah Mysticism and Talmudic Tradition* (New York: Jewish Theological Seminary of America, 1960), pp. 118–126.

11. See Moshe Idel, *Kabbalah: New Perspectives,* p. 223.

12. *Makkot* 11a.

13. *Kiddushin* 71a; *Pesaḥim* 50a.

14. Naḥmanides, *Perushei ha-Torah* (ed. Chavel), Introduction, p. 6.

15. This is cited in J. Dan, *Torat ha-Sod shel Ḥasidei Ashkenaz,* pp. 122–126; see also Gershom Scholem, *Kitvei Yad ba-Kabbalah* (Jerusalem, 1930), pp. 213–217.

16. See TZ 13a, 19a, 26a, 40b, 100b, 104a, 130b; cf. *Sefer ha-Kanah* (Cracow 1894) 88a–b, *Sefer ha-Peliah* (Koreẓ 1883), 53d. See also *Sefer Pardes Rimmonim, Sha'ar Peratei ha-Shemot,* 12–13. See also Z I 204a, TZ 40b, 160a.

17. RM II 42b; TZ 64b.

18. RM III 257b–258a. This idea seems to draw heavily on the Maimonidean negative theology, that God is known through His actions rather than through his essence; cf. *The Guide for the Perplexed* 1:50–59.

19. RM III 257b.

20. TZ 61a; RM III 230a.

21. *'Avodah Zarah* 8a, 42b; *Sanhedrin* 56b; see TZ 89a, 97b.

22. See RM III 228a, 250b; TZ 13b, 41b. The latter deals with language, especially the five consonantal families and their respective energies. See also TZḤ 104d, 115d, 120b; TZ 4a–b, 16a.

23. *Berakhot* 55a; see also Jubilees 36: 7.

24. See Elliot Wolfson, "Biblical Accentuation in a Kabbalistic Key: Mystical Interpretation of the Ta'amim," *Journal of Jewish Liturgy and Music* (1988–1990) 21: 1–15; 22:1–13; Yehudah Liebes, *Peraqim be-Millon Sefer ha-Zohar,* pp. 174–175.

25. TZḤ 101a; TZ 20b, 45a–51b; RM III 247b.

26. TZ 108a. See also 39b, 40b, 104b, 105a.

27. As in "*karnei farah* ("The bull's horns," a paired set of notes.) are the two true prophets" (TZ 48a).

28. See particularly TZ 7b, 9b, 104b.

29. TZ 5a.

30. TZ 42b.

31. TZ 8a, 26b, 61b.

32. TZ 4a, 55a 61b, 109b; TZḤ 100a, 113b, 106b. See Elliot Wolfson, "Biblical Accentuation in a Kabbalistic Key;" Part 2, pp. 8–9; Yehudah Liebes, "Hashpa'ot Noẓriot 'al Sefer ha-Zohar" [Christian Influences on the Zohar], *Jerusalem Studies in Jewish Thought* 2, no. 1, (1982–1983): 54–56.

33. *Berakhot* 35b. See Saul Lieberman, *Hellenism in Jewish Palestine* (New York: Jewish Theological Seminary 1950), pp. 49–51. Lieberman considered the *ein . . . ella* formula to be one of the earliest strata of Rabbinic exegesis, which lost its literal function in later aggadic usages.

34. RM III 82a: *ein aviv ella kudsha-berikh-hu.*

35. RM III 242a, after *Berakhot* 26b.

36. RM III 243a–R. Shimon said: "this is *you*"; i.e., Hod; RM III 243a—"*La-menaẓeaḥ* is the masters-of-victory" (literally the *sefirah neẓaḥ*).

37. RM III 178b.

38. RM III 108b,115a; TZ 15b, 54b.

39. TZ 19a.

40. TZ 21b.

41. TZ 10a, 35a.

42. See *Baba Batra* 25b; RM III 253b, 257a. See also Chapter 5 of this study, "Prayer as Unification."

43. TZḤ 103c.

44. Cf. Rashi, *Sanhedrin,* 56a: "when someone reverses his words in order not to curse or blaspheme, this is *kinnui,* in the language of the sages." *Shavuot,* 35a, 36a, implies that the attributes of God are also *kinnuyim,* see also *Tamid* 33b, *Tosafot* to *Sotah,* 38a.

45. An apparent exception is a section of the Zohar Ḥadash 40d, in a commentary to the *Merkavah* (my thanks to Elliot Wolfson for pointing this out): "All the *kinnuyim* of names are dependent on the secret of the Holy Name. These are called the hidden beings that cover the inner names, flying over some and covering others. . . . From the lower firmament hang the *kinnuyim.* Above it there are no *kinnuyim.* . . . In the world to come the secret of the Holy Name will not be hidden in these, but will be known openly and not through *kinnuyim."*

46. See Jacob Klatzkin, *Oẓar ha-Munaḥim ha-Philosophiyim* [The Treasury of Philosophical Terms] vol. 2 (Berlin: Eshkol, 1928), pp. 96–97.

47. 1:65.

48. 5:2.

49. Ms. Vatican 266, f.44a:1. "The Hebrew Paraphrase of Sa'adiah Gaon's Kitab al-Amanat wa'l I'tiqadat" *A.J.S. Review* 11, no. 1 (Spring 1986).

50. *Sha'arei Orah,* 2a, see Gershom Scholem, *On the Kabbalah and Its Symbolism,* p. 42. Gikatilla's earlier work, *Ginnat Egoz,* also contains considerable reference to *kinnuyim;* see *Sefer Ginnat Egoz* (Jerusalem: Yeshivat ha-Ḥaggim ve-ha-Shalom, 1989) p. 518.

51. Cf. Maimonides's *The Guide for the Perplexed,* 1:50–59.

52. TZ 1a.

53. TZ 11a; see *Sanhedrin,* 56a; *Shavuot,* 36a.

54. RM III 215b.

55. See Z II 118a, III 21b, 27b, 185b, 269b. See also Naḥmanides's commentary on Deuteronomy 3:24.

56. RM III 257b. See also RM III 253a; TZ 14b, 15a; TZḤ 103a.

57. Ibid.

58. *Sefer Pardes Rimmonim,* 106a.

59. Literally, permutations of the ineffable name YHVH, with *Elohim*, a central biblical name for God.

60. TZḤ 101a.

61. I (TZ) 22b.

62. TZ 60b.

63. RM III 238b.

Chapter Three Notes

1. RM III 124b.

2. 12:3.

3. See TZ 1a, 10a–b, 13a–b, 14a, 16a, 17a; TZḤ 99c, 103a, 104b, 105c, 106b, 107d, 117c–d; RM III 249a. The text provided by Moshe Cordovero in *Or Yaqar: Tiqqunei ha-Zohar* consists of all these texts in combination. Certainly TZḤ 93d–94b seems to be an early draft of TZ 1a–2b.

4. Z I 15a, 100a (*Sitrei Torah*), 113b and 116a (*Midrash ha-Ne'elam*), 130a; II 2a and 23a.

5. Z I 113b.

6. Z I 116a.

7. This is a reference to the supernal *sefirah Binah,* which is supported by the intermediate *sefirot*. These serve as a conduit through which Divine effluence flows to the practitioner.

8. Z I 15b; more conventionally in I 130b: "The *ẓaddikim* know the master's secret and cleave to him." See Elliot Wolfson, "The Hermeneutics of Visionary Experience," p. 330n.

9. TZḤ 106b.

10. Cf. *Or Yaqar: Tiqqunei ha-Zohar,* II, p. 97.

11. TZḤ 105c. Yehudah Liebes, in *Peraqim be-Millon Sefer ha-Zohar,* p. 175, identifies a preceding section in TZḤ 104c as part of the composition *Sitrei Torah.* Elliot Wolfson maintains that this statement originates with the author of the main part of the Zohar, following the form of the *Matnitin* compositions.

12. TZ 74a; TZḤ 115b; RM III 82a.

13. TZḤ 106b.

14. See Z I 15b.

15. TZḤ 105c, 106b.

16. TZḤ 107d.

17. TZḤ 104b.

18. Cf. Cordovero, in *Or ha-Ḥamah,* II, 27a: "seeing the thing within the thing." Also Galante, ibid., 15b, "The secret of wisdom,

the inner wisdom, the secret of the root of the verses through the *sefirot*."

19. Z II 23a

20. TZ 31b; RM II 158b, III 222b, 232a. The Zohar's equation of the mystical hermeneutic with prophecy has been noted by Elliot Wolfson, in "The Hermeneutics of Visionary Experience," pp. 311–345. See also RM III 110a.

21. TZ 40b.

22. TZ 75a, 80a.

23. *Sukkot* 45b.

24. III 110a; TZ 69b, 75a.

25. Hebrew: *davar,* meaning word or thing.

26. TZḤ 105c. See note 13.

27. *Sefer Pardes Rimmonim,* 105b.

28. Ibid., 105b.

29. "The Name of God and Linguistic Theory of the Kaballah," p. 165.

30. RM III 124a.

31. TZḤ 99c, 103a.

32. TZ 2a.

33. TZḤ 94a.

34. TZḤ 99c, TZḤ 103a.

35. *Berakhot,* 3b.

36. TZ 2a.

37. RM III 124b.

38. "Ha-Reqa' ha-Histori shel ha-*Ra'aya Meheimna*" [The Historical Context of the *Ra'aya Meheimna*] *Zion* 5 (1940): 16.

39. RM III 124b, 153b. See Liebes, *Peraqim be-Millon Sefer ha-Zohar,* p. 118.

40. *Babba Batra* 75a; TZ 136b; see Reuven Margoliot, *Niẓoẓei Zohar,* note 9.

41. Alternatively; *understanding.* See *Tamid,* 32a, "Who is wise? He who sees the impending." Hagigah 14a, "Who is understanding (*navon*)? He who understands the inner aspect." Cf. ZḤ 44d; TZ 98a.

42. Literally *zahara.*

43. TZḤ 103d.

44. TZḤ 104d.

45. RM III 111a–b.

46. I (TZ) 24a; RM II 119a, 229b; TZ 6a, 23b, 41b, 80a, 99b, 100a, 102b. One antecedent is from *Bereshit Rabbah,* 1:4: *Israel was conceived in thought* (before Creation). See also Z II 108b.

47. TZ 6a, 43a, 125b, 141b.

48. See *Ozar ha-Zohar,* pp. 645–652. See also Arthur Green, "The Zaddiq as *Axis Mundi," Journal of the American Academy of Religion* 45, no. 3 (1977): 332–337; *Tormented Master: A Life of Rabbi Naḥman of Bratzlav* (Tuscaloosa: University of Alabama Press, 1979), p. 132n.

49. Aramaic: *de-leit leih mi-di-leih.*

50. TZ 58a. See also Moshe Cordovero, *Sefer Pardes Rimmonim,* II, 34b; Green, *Tormented Master,* pp. 41, 57n.

51. RM II 115b, 158b.

52. *Nedarim,* 41b; TZ 5b, 66b.

53. *Berakhot,* 54a; TZ 10b, 84b, RM III 33b, 279a.

54. *Nedarim,* 64b; RM II 119a; TZ 66b.

55. TZḤ 107a.

56. TZ 10b.

57. TZ 2a, also I (TZ) 28b. See Amos Goldreich, "La'az Iberi be-fragment bilti-yadu'a shel Ba'al *Tiqqunei ha-Zohar* ," pp. 110, 119; also Yehudah Liebes, *Peraqim be-Millon Sefer ha-Zohar,* p. 219.

58. "Ha-Reqa' ha-Histori shel ha-*Ra'aya Meheimna,"* pp. 10, 18–19, 30; *A History of the Jews in Christian Spain,* vol. 1, trans. by Louis Schoffman (Philadelphia: Jewish Publication Society, l978), pp. 270–277. See especially RM III 273b.

59. *A History of the Jews in Christian Spain,* p. 277. See also Liebes, *Peraqim be-Millon Sefer ha-Zohar,* p. 48; also Gershom Scholem, *Sabbatai Ṣevi: The Mystical Messiah* (Princeton, N.J.: Bollingen, 1973), pp. 746–747.

60. Tishby, MhZ *II,* pp. 697–702.

61. Ibid, p. 699.

62. Ibid, p. 702.

63. "La'az Iberi be-fragment Bilti-Yadu'a shel Ba'al *Tiqqunei ha-Zohar,"* p. 107.

64. TZḤ 111d.

65. *Avot* 1:13; RM II 116a, III 29a, 244a; TZ 5b, 11b, 25a, 61b; TZḤ 100a, 106c; see also Z I 42a. Gershom Scholem argued for the theurgic nature of this remark in Merkavah tradition; see *Jewish Gnosticism, Merkabah Mysticism and Talmudic Tradition,* pp. 80–81.

66. TZ 11b.

67. TZ 25a, 61a–b, 20b.

68. See *Be'er La-ḥai Ro'i* on TZ 25a. See also Elliot Wolfson, "Female Imaging of the Torah: From Literary Metaphor to Religious Symbol," in *From Ancient Israel to Modern Judaism: Intellect in Quest of*

Understanding: Essays in Honor of Marvin Fox, vol. 2 (Atlanta: Scholars Press, 1990), pp. 298–299.

69. As in *tashmish ha-mitah* (literally, "use of the bed," i.e., sexual relations).

70. *Megillah,* 28b.

71. RM III 244a.

72. RM III 29b; TZ 5b.

73. TZ 142b.

74. Z II 9a; III 178b, 270a.

75. TZ 5b.

76. *Avot* 1:3.

77. TZḤ 107a; RM III 109a.

78. RM III 29a; TZḤ 106c.

79. RM II 90a, 119a; III 83a, 109a, 277b; TZ 131a, 146b, 179b; TZḤ (TZ) 31a.

80. This theme reappeared in early Ḥasidism; see Arthur Green, *Tormented Master,* pp. 229, 267n.

81. TZ 1b, 53a, 93b; RM III 111b, 125b–126a.

Chapter Four Notes

1. Beẓalel Safran, "Rabbi Azriel and Naḥmanides," in Isadore Twersky, ed., *Rabbi Moses Naḥmanides (Ramban): Explorations in His Religious and Literary Virtuosity* (Cambridge, Mass.: Harvard University Press, 1983), p. 75.

2. See Alexander Altmann, "The Gnostic Background of the Rabbinic Adam Legends," in *Studies in Religious Philosophy and Mysticism* (Ithaca, N.Y.: Cornell University Press, 1969), pp. 1–16, 161–179; Joseph Dan, "Samael, Lilith and the Concept of Evil in Early Kabbalah," *AJS Review* 5 (1980): 17–41; Yehudah Liebes, *Peraqim be-Millon Sefer ha-Zohar,* p. 83; Shulamit Shaḥar, "Ha-Catarism ve-Reshit ha-Qabbalah be-Lanquedoc" [Catharism and the Beginnings of the Kabbalah in Lanquedoc], *Tarbiẓ 40* (1971): 483–507.

3. In the classical midrash, see *Bereshit Rabbah,* 3:7, 9:2; *Qohelet Rabbah,* 3:11; *Shoḥer Tov,* 34:1. In the Zohar, see I 154b, 262b; III 135a–b, 292b. In the *Tiqqunim,* see I (TZ) 24b, 252b–253a; III 61a, 292b; TZḤ 108a, 110a–b, 114b–d. See also Joseph Dan, "No Evil Descends from Heaven," in Bernard Dov Cooperman, ed. *Jewish Thought in the Sixteenth Century* (Cambridge, Mass.: Harvard University Press, 1983), pp. 94–97; Yehudah Liebes, "Ha-Mashiaḥ shel ha-Zohar," p. 219; Isaiah Tishby, *Netivei Emunah u-Minut* [Paths of Faith

and Heresy] (Jerusalem: Magnes Press, 1982), pp. 25–29; "Hashpa'ot Nozriot 'al Sefer ha-Zohar," p. 52.

4. Z I (TZ) 25a; TZ 40a, 99b, 100a, 102b, 112a, 114a. See *Qohelet Rabbah,* 1:4.

5. TZ 99b, 119a.

6. *Shabbat,* 146a; *Avodah Zarah,* 22b; *Yevamot,* 103b.

7. *Bahir,* 199.

8. Z I 36b, 37a, 52b, 122b, 126a, 145b, 253b; II 231a; III 76b, 143a, 161a; TZḤ 58d, 63c.

9. I (TZ) 28b; TZ 93a, 99b, 100a, 113b, 117a, 129a; TZḤ (TZ) 31c, 33d.

10. TZ 66a.

11. TZ 94a.

12. TZ 24a.

13. *Sanhedrin,* 38b.

14. Z I 38b.

15. TZ 99b, 100a, 116b, 128b; TZḤ 114c.

16. Reuven Margaliot, *Sha'arei ha-Zohar* (Jerusalem: Mossad ha-Rav Kook, 1978), p. 190.

17. Z I 35b.

18. TZḤ (TZ) 33c.

19. This makes use of the biblical terms *Gai, Nashi, Ẓiyah, Arka, Ereẓ, Adamah, Tevel.*

20. An expression associated, in the Midrash, with the descent into the underworld; see *Rosh ha-Shanah,* 17a.

21. TZḤ (TZ) 33c–d.

22. TZḤ (TZ) 33d.

23. TZ 115a–b; TZḤ 110b; I (TZ) 23a; *Bahir,* 200. See also Altmann, "The Gnostic Background of the Rabbinic Adam Legends," pp. 1–16; Moshe Idel, *Kabbalah: New Perspectives,* pp. 117–119, 131, 183, 330n; Gershom Scholem, *Kabbalah,* p. 164.

24. TZ 115a.

25. Literally, "the Cause of Causes," a reference to *Keter 'Elyon,* the highest level of the Godhead.

26. TZ 115a.

27. TZ 115a–b.

28. This is also found in Meir ibn Sahula. See Bezalel Safran "Rabbi Azriel and Naḥmanides," p. 89n; also Baḥya ben Asher's *Commentary to the Torah* (Chavel ed. vol. 2), p. 556.

29. RM III 124b.

30. I (TZ) 26b; RM III 98a–b, 124a–125a, 153a, 252b–253a, 255a; TZḤ 106c. See also Gershom Scholem, *On the Kabbalah and Its*

Symbolism, pp. 79, 109; *Sabbatai Ṣevi,* pp. 11, 809, 811, 818; Amos Goldreich, "La'az Iberi be-Fragment Bilti-Yadu'a shel Ba'al *Tiqqunei ha-Zohar,"* p. 96n.

31. TZḤ 107a; RM II 118b–119a.

32. I (TZ) 27a; TZ 78a.

33. RM III 98a–b.

34. RM III 274b.

35. RM III 255a.

36. TZ 64b.

37. RM III 98a–b.

38. TZ 60a.

39. As in the Z I 35a: "all the waters of creation branch out from beneath it."

40. RM III 124b. This is apparently based on Z I 35a: "The Tree of Knowledge of Good and Evil suckles from both sides, and knows them as one knows both the sweet and the bitter . . . "

41. TZḤ 107a, after *Baba Batra,* 8a; RM III 247a.

42. Hebrew *yeẓer.*

43. Heb. *va-yiẓer,* a play on *yeẓer.* For antecedents, see *Berakhot,* 61a; *Bereshit Rabbah,* 14:2.

44. TZḤ 106c.

45. "Ha-Reqa' ha-Histori shel ha-*Ra'aya Meheimna,"* p. 23.

46. As in "to cut the shoot."

47. TZḤ 106c.

48. TZ 87a; cf. *Avot,* 3:22. Two broad assessments of the phenomenon of the World Tree are Gerhart B. Ladner, "Medieval and Modern Understandings of Symbolism: A Comparison," *Speculum* 54 (1979): 223–257; and David Bynum, *The Daemon in the Wood* (Cambridge, Mass.: Harvard University Press, 1978).

49. TZ 60a.

50. TZ 128b.

51. See TZ 64a.

52. TZḤ 120c; also TZ 128b; RM III 230a; 235b. See also *Berakhot,* 28a.

53. TZ 82b; RM III 223b.

54. *Baba Batra,* 73b; RM III 223b; TZ 2b.

55. TZ 53a–b; RM III 278b.

56. TZḤ 94a.

57. RM III 153b.

58. TZ 55a. Similarly, birds are employed to symbolize the soul (TZ 23a; see also Z I 199a), the animation of talmudic discourse (RM III 228a), or the angelic realm (TZ 2b, 23a, 83a; RM III 227a).

Finally, various typologies of religious behavior are developed, based on the commandments regarding the taking of the mother bird with her young (RM III 216a, 254a–b).

59. TZ 53a–54b.

60. TZ 9a, 136b.

61. TZ 53b; RM III 222b.

62. RM II 120b.

63. Yiẓḥak Baer, *A History of the Jews in Christian Spain,* I, p. 270.

64. Yiẓḥak Baer, "Ha-Reqa' ha-Histori shel ha-*Ra'aya Meheimna,"* pp. 10–11, 15.

65. Tishby, *MhZ* II, p. 393. See also Z I 67b, III 14b; TZ 54b.

66. TZ 33a, 54b.

67. This practice is noted in the prefaces of Shalom Buzaglo to the commentary *Kisse Melekh,* Elijah of Vilna to the *Biur ha-GR"A,* and in the publisher's introduction to the second edition (Orta Koj).

68. Tishby, *MhZ* I pp. 285–307.

69. It is not the purpose of this book to exhaustively review the most important aspects of recent research on this subject. It is extensively treated in Joseph Dan, "Samael, Lillit and the Concept of Evil in Early Kabbalah"; Mikhal Oron, "Qabbalat Castilea—Hemshekh O Mahapeḥah?" [The Kabbalah in Castile—Continuation or Revolution?"], *Jerusalem Studies in Jewish Thought* 6: 383–392; Shulamit Shaḥar, "Catharism and the Beginnings of the Kabbalah in Lanquedoc"; Gershom Scholem, *Origins of the Kabbalah,* pp. 292–298; "Hitpatḥut Torat ha-'Olamot" [The Development of the Tradition of the Worlds], *Tarbiẓ* 2: 415–442; 3: 33–66; *Pirqei Yesod be-Havanat ha-Qabbalah u-Semaleha* [Essential Chapters in the Understanding of the Kabbalah and Its Symbolism] (Jerusalem, 1976), pp. 191–193; Elliot Wolfson, "Left Contained in Right: A Study in Zoharic Hermeneutics," *Association for Jewish Studies Journal* 11 (1987); "Light Through Darkness: The Ideal of Human Perfection in the Zohar," *Harvard Theological Review* 81 (1988): 78–84. See also Tishby, *MhZ* I, pp. 285–307.

70. As portrayed by Elliot Wolfson "Left Contained in Right," pp. 27–32.

71. Gershom Scholem, *Origins of the Kabbalah,* pp. 292–298.

72. Shulamit Shaḥar "Catharism and the Beginnings of the Kabbalah in Lanquedoc," p. 502.

73. Z II 148b.

74. Z I 167a, 194a, III 41b, 70a.

75. See Naḥmanides's commentary on Leviticus 17:7; Scholem, *Kabbalah,* p. 320; also Tishby, *MhZ* I, pp. 150–151, 296.

76. Z I 16a; II 112a.

77. TZ 111a.

78. TZ 95a.

79. *Berakhot,* 17a; RM II 40b; III 232b, 237b; TZ 100a.

80. Z I 35a–36b, 238b, 240a.

81. TZ 14b, 24a, 92b; I (TZ) 29a; Scholem, *Kabbalah,* pp. 385–388.

82. TZ 96a. This is Adam's first wife, after the *Alpha-Beta de-Ben Sira.* See Gershom Scholem *Sabbatai Ṣevi,* p. 228; Erich Neumann, *The Great Mother* (Princeton, N.J.: Bollingen, 1955), pp. 147–174.

83. I (TZ) 27b, after Leviticus 18:16: "the nakedness of a woman and her daughter."

84. See Scholem, *Kabbalah,* pp. 358–359, Moshe Idel, *Kabbalah: New Perspectives,* pp. 166–167.

85. RM III 253a. See also 277a; Scholem, *Kabbalah,* pp. 320–326.

86. RM III 277a.

87. TZ 9a; RM II 117b; III 247a. See also Z I 178b; *Sukkah,* 52a.

88. TZḤ 107c; see *Yoma,* 69b.

89. TZ 98b; see Z II 106b.

90. RM III 179a; see also 277a; TZ 37a.

91. TZ 60a; RM III 124a; see Scholem, *Kabbalah,* pp. 385–388. In a recently published fragment by the author of the *Tiqqunim,* there is a brief excursus on the relationship of Satan and the *yeẓer ha-ra'* (Amos Goldreich, "La'az Iberi be-fragment Bilti-Yadu'a shel Ba'al *Tiqqunei ha-Zohar,"* p. 98), although Goldreich expresses some doubt about the passage's authenticity (ibid., p. 115).

92. 41b; see *Berakhot,* 61b.

93. TZ 133a; RM III 247a.

94. TZḤ 116a.

95. "Who is mighty? He who overcomes his impulse" (*Avot* 4:1).

96. TZ 119b, TZḤ 118d, see Sukkah 52b.

97. I (TZ) 27b; TZ 27b, 53b, 95b, 112b, 140a. See also Scholem, *Sabbatai Ṣevi* pp. 741–742, Goldreich, "La'az Iberi be-fragment bilti-yadu'a shel Ba'al *Tiqqunei ha-Zohar,"* pp. 107–109; Tishby, *MhZ II,* pp. 686–687.

98. RM III 282a.

99. RM III 232a.

100. RM III 125b.

101. TZ 27b.

102. I (TZ) 25a; RM III 282b; TZ 55a, 86a; see *Bereshit Rabbah,* 26:7.

103. Yiẓḥak Baer identified allusions to social and historical phenomena of the reigns of Alfonso X and Sancho IV in the *Ra'aya Meheimna* and *Tiqqunim* (*A History of the Jews in Christian Spain* vol. 1, p. 244). See also Scholem, *Sabbatai Ṣevi,* pp. 71, 746.

104. TZḤ 117a.

105. RM III 153a; TZ 44b.

106. *Avot,* 2:5. See also TZ 5b, 6a; TZḤ 107a; RM III 33b.

107. TZ 6a.

108. *Shabbat,* 22a.

109. RM III 279a.

110. RM III 277a.

111. RM III 277a–b.

112. RM III 125a.

113. Ibid.

114. Yiẓḥak Baer, "Ha-Reqa' ha-histori shel ha-*Ra'aya Meheimna,*" pp. 5, 9. See also Ronald Kiener, "The Image of Islam in the Zohar," in Joseph Dan, ed., *The Zohar and Its Generation,* pp. 43–66; Bernard Septimus, "Taḥat Edom ve-lo Taḥat Yishmael—Gilgulo Shel Maamar" [Better Under Edom than Ishmael—The Transformation of an Expression], *Zion* 47 (1982): 103–111.

115. TZḤ 121a; RM III 219a; 237a 246b; Jacob Neusner, *What Is Midrash?* p. 53; Gershom Scholem, *Origins of the Kabbalah,* p. 296.

116. See Wilhelm Bacher, "Judaeo-Christian Polemics in the Zohar," *Jewish Quarterly Review* 3 (1891): 781–784; Yehudah Liebes, "Hashpa'ot Noẓriot 'al Sefer ha-Zohar," pp. 43–74.

117. RM III 278b, 280a; See also Baer, "Ha-Reqa' ha-histori shel ha-*Ra'aya Meheimna,*" p. 28; *A History of the Jews in Christian Spain,* vol. 1, p. 277; Scholem, *Major Trends in Jewish Mysticism,* pp. 229–230; Arthur Green, *Tormented Master: A Life of Rabbi Nahman of Bratzlav,* pp. 187–188, 215n–216n.

118. RM III 278b.

119. TZ 113a: "His influence extends through every generation," 114a: "Moses extends through every generation, in every *ẓaddik;*" cf. *Shabbat* 101b; *Shir ha-Shirim Rabbah, 1:4,* 7–8; TZ 112a, 114a. See also Scholem, *Sabbatai Ṣevi,* pp. 53, 56. See also Liebes, "The Messiah of the Zohar," pp. 90n, 105–107, 112; Elliot Wolfson, "The Hermeneutics of Visionary Experience," pp. 339n, 344–345n.

120. Cf. *Yerushalmi Sanhedrin,* 4:2. The charged nature of the number forty-nine appears throughout the Zohar and *Tiqqunim*; see TZ 7b; RM II 115a.

121. *Shir ha-Shirim Rabbah,* 1.

122. TZ 111b–112a.

123. TZ 71b.

124. RM III 125b, 280a ; I (TZ) 27b, 28a; *Sotah,* 13b. See also Scholem, *Kabbalah,* p. 191.

125. Scholem, *Origins of the Kabbalah,* pp. 163, 168–176

126. RM III 28a; see also Z III 4b.

127. RM III 281a.

128. TZ 22b.

129. TZ 18a, 65b, 92a.

130. TZ 94b.

131. TZ 73b.

132. TZḤ 102d.

133. TZ 60a, 73a.

134. TZḤ 117a; RM III 277a.

135. TZ 98a–b.

136. TZ 93b.

137. TZ 19b, 28b, 56a. This tradition is further explicated by Ḥayyim Vital, *Peri Eẓ Ḥayyim: Festival of Maẓẓot,* pp. 3, 7. (Jerusalem: Kabbalah Research Center 1964).

138. TZ 30b.

139. TZ 28b; Z II 182b on the recitation of *Hallel.*

140. Tishby, *MhZ* I, pp.112–117; Scholem, *Kabbalah,* p. 148.

141. "Hitpatḥut Torat ha'olamot," pp. 46, 59, 67

142. In only three places: I 177b; II 155; II 192b.

143. Scholem, *Kabbalah,* pp. 88–89.

144. "Hitpatḥut Torat ha-'Olamot," p. 82.

145. RM II 42b–43a

146. TZ 3b.

147. TZ 42a, 98b; I (TZ) 22a.

148. In TZḤ (TZ) 33c.

149. See Idel, *Kabbalah: New Perspectives,* pp. 136–146; Scholem, *Kabbalah,* p. 102.

150. TZ 3b, 68b, 88a; RM II 42b, III 258a. See Daniel Matt, *Zohar—The Book of Enlightenment* (Ramsey, N.J.: Paulist Press, 1981), pp. 33–37.

151. II 42b-43a.

152. TZḤ (TZ) 32d; RM III 225a.

153. TZ 91b–92a, 98b.
154. TZ 17a; RM III 257b–258a.
155. RM III 258a; TZ 42a.
156. I (TZ) 22b.
157. Tishby, MhZ I, p. 11.

Chapter Five Notes

1. TZ 14b, 44a, 58a; RM III 153a.
2. TZ 4b–5a; TZḤ 106c–107a. See Liebes, *Peraqim be-Millon Sefer ha-Zohar,* pp. 119, 124.
3. TZ 44a, 98b; RM III 124a–126a.
4. Contemporary understandings of the primordial Torah are to be found in Azriel of Gerona, *Perush ha-Aggadot le-Rabbeinu Azriel,* ed. I Tishby (Jerusalem, 1945); 101–102. See also Bezalel Safran, "Rabbi Azriel and Naḥmanides," in Twersky, ed., *Rabbi Moses Naḥmanides (Ramban),* p. 77.
5. *Eruvin,* 100a.
6. Aramaic: *Saba, Saba.*
7. *Avot,* 1:13.
8. TZḤ 106c.
9. TZ 6b, 64a; I (TZ) 23a–b; RM III 215b.
10. RM III 82b–83a.
11. Ibid.
12. TZ 46a–b, 58a, 145a.
13. *On the Kabbalah and Its Symbolism,* pp. 56–57, 66–70; *Sabbatai Ṣevi,* pp. 11, 809, 811, 818.
14. See Scholem, *Sabbatai Ṣevi,* pp. 11–12, 53, 59, 72, 228, 741–742.
15. "Ha-Reqa' ha-histori shel ha-*Ra'aya Meheimna,*" pp. 35, 39.
16. Tishby, MhZ II, pp. 375–397.
17. Ibid., p. 375.
18. Ibid., p. 395 (English translation by David Goldstein, *The Wisdom of the Zohar* [Oxford: University Press, 1989], pp. 1109, 1112.
19. I (TZ) 27a–28a; RM III 27b, 124b, 153a–b; TZ 82a; TZḤ 97c.
20. See Frank Talmage, "Apples of Gold: The Inner Meaning of Sacred Texts in Medieval Judaism": 319–321; Gershom Scholem, *On the Kabbalah and Its Symbolism,* p. 61*; Kabbalah,* pp. 172–173.
21. Literally, "proofs."
22. Literally, "the mouth teaching laws."
23. TZḤ 102d, 105c–d; RM III 110a. In I (TZ) 26b, the levels are described as *peshatim, ra'ayot, derashot,* and *sitrei Torah.*

24. RM III 29b.
25. RM III 223b.
26. TZ 145a.
27. An acronym for *Torah she-be-al peh;* literally, "Oral Torah."
28. Literally, "we learned."
29. Literally, "according to a system."
30. Literally, "answer."
31. Literally, "extraneous Tannaitic material."
32. Popularly understood as an acronym for *Tishby ye'tareẓ qushyot u'va'ayot,* implying that in the messianic age, "the Tishbite (i.e., Elijah) will resolve questions and problems."
33. Literally, "question."
34. Literally, "stricture."
35. Literally, "leniency."
36. TZḤ 99a.
37. RM II 120b.
38. TZḤ 98d.
39. TZḤ 107a–b
40. See this study, pp. 27–30, 46–48.
41. TZḤ 106d. *Ḥamor,* "donkey," is understood as an acronym for *ḥakham mufla ve-rav Rabbanan,* "wondrously wise, a Rabbi of Rabbis." See Scholem, *Kabbalah,* p. 191, also Tishby, MhZ II, p. 385.
42. This text is also interpreted in RM III 124a; TZ 22a, 52a, 140a. See also *Avodah Zarah,* 17a.
43. Avot, 2:16.
44. TZḤ 97c.
45. An argument from a minor premise to a major.
46. In RM III 153a: *"with all the work in the field,* that is *'Teyqu.'* "
47. I (TZ) 27a. See also RM III 153a–b, 229b; TZḤ 97c–d.
48. TZ 43a.
49. TZḤ 99d; see also 46a.
50. TZ 46a, 82a.
51. TZ 46a
52. An apparent reference to the *Shekhinah.*
53. TZ 46a.
54. RM III 229b, 278b–279a. From Jeremiah 23:29: *Are not my words like fire and like a hammer breaking a rock?* See *Shabbat,* 88b: *Just as the hammer gives off many sparks, so every word uttered by the Blessed Holy One was divided into seventy languages.*
55. RM III 279b. See also TZ 44a, TZḤ 98b.
56. TZḤ 98b.
57. I (TZ) 27b–28a.

58. RM III 279a.

59. Though the author of the *Tiqqunim* did not demur from making such predictions himself! See Goldreich "La'az Iberi be-Fragment Bilti-Yadu'a shel Ba'al *Tiqqunei ha-Zohar,*" p. 91n.

60. *Hagigah,* 14b; also *Tosefta Hagigah,* 2:2; *Song of Songs Rabbah,* 1:4. Gershom Scholem demonstrated, through readings of other *Heikhalot* texts that have subsequently come to light, that the passage refers to a particular peril at the sixth station of the mystic's ascent. Ephraim Urbach argued for the most oblique rendering of the account being the true basis for analysis. Cf. Ira Chernus, *Mysticism in Rabbinic Judaism,* p. 2; Scholem, *Jewish Gnosticism, Merkabah Mysticism and Talmudic Tradition,* pp. 14–19; Joseph Dan, "The Religious Experience of the Merkavah," in Green, ed., *Jewish Spirituality,* vol. 1, pp. 292–294; Moshe Idel, *Kabbalah: New Perspectives,* p. 183; David Halperin, *The Faces of the Chariot* (Tubingen: J. C. B. Mohr, 1988), pp. 31–37.

61. With the exception of the *Heikhalot* accounts: II 254b. Elliot Wolfson has reminded me that the *Pardes* account's term for "entered and exiting," *'al u-nefaq,* is widespread in the main sections of the Zohar.

62. I (TZ) 26b; TZ 11b, 69a, 80b, 88b; TZḤ 107c.

63. RM III 246b, 258a.

64. See above, :pp. 69–70

65. TZ 88b.

66. Belly, in Hebrew: *gaḥon.*

67. Hebrew: *ḥad qal.*

68. Hebrew: *pirya ve-rivya.*

69. I (TZ) 26b. See also TZ 88a.

70. I (TZ) 26b.

71. TZ 11b.

72. *Hagigah,* 15b

73. TZ 11b, 69a–b. See also *Hagigah,* 11b, 14b; Z II 254b (*Heikhalot*). In the *Tiqqunim:* Z I (TZ) 26b; RM III 223b; TZ 11b, 69a, 88b. TZ 92b also deals with the process of transcending the *qelippot* in a manner not unrelated to the *Pardes.*

74. TZ 69a–b.

75. TZ 114a.

76. TZ 102a.

77. TZḤ 107c; TZ 11a–b, I (TZ) 26a–27a.

78. Yehudah Liebes ("Keiẓad Nitḥabber Sefer ha-Zohar?": 13 in J. Dan; ed. *The Zohar and its Generation, Jerusalem Studies in Jewish Thought 8* (Jerusalem: Magnes 1989) maintains that the *Ra'aya*

Meheimna used the term *Masters of the Mishnah* only for remarks that it considered authentically talmudic.

79. RM III 278a, also 42a.

80. Correlated with the forty-nine letters of "Hear O Israel . . . ," and "Blessed be His Glorious Name . . . ," the central Jewish prayer. See *Eruvin,* 13b.

81. Literally, *mishneh la-melekh.*

82. TZ 14a–b.

83. TZ 14b.

84. See Halperin, *The Faces of the Chariot,* pp. 420–426; Scholem, *Jewish Gnosticism, Merkabah Mysticism and Talmudic Tradition,* pp. 49–50.

85. TZ 14b

86. RM III 228a; TZḤ 107b.

87. I (TZ) 252b.

88. TZ 43a; TZḤ 98a.

89. TZ 14b, 46a, 147a.

90. TZḤ 112a; see RM III 29b; TZ 14a.

91. The idea of ten *sefirot* within each *sefirah* occurs in TZ 84a, 116b, 125b, 135a.

92. TZḤ 108a; TZ 5a-b, 14b, 48b, 199a.

93. TZ 75a, 80a, 147a.

94. TZ 82a; this remark forms the basis for Moshe Cordovero's initial homily in his popular work *Or Ne'erav,* 1:1.

95. Literally, *gan,* whose numerical coefficicent is fifty-three.

96. TZ 38a.

97. RM III 257a. See also Goldreich, "La'az Iberi be-Fragment Bilti-Yadu'a shel Ba'al *Tiqqunei ha-Zohar,*" p. 103.

98. RM III 230a.

99. TZ 11b; RM III 42a.

100. RM III 124b.

101. TZ 19b; TZḤ 116b; I (TZ) 252b, after *Avot,* 5:16.

102. The Zoharic literature is intensely erotic, yet its eroticism is tinged with darkness. The prevalence of erotic metaphor serves only to emphasize a terror of its illicitness. This charged quality may betray a morbid sexual pathology in remarks such as "a cohen has to take a virgin, because otherwise she's a used cup, since the woman is the cup of blessing" (RM III 89b). Yehudah Liebes speculates intriguingly on the possibility of sexual dysfunction on the part of the author of the Zohar ("Ha-Mashiaḥ shel ha-Zohar," pp. 203–205).

In both the Zohar and the *Tiqqunim,* there are references to the corrupting and demonic nature of intercourse with a menstruous woman, a maidservant, a gentile woman, or a prostitute (respectively, *Niddah, Shifḥah, Goyah, Zonah;* acronym *Nashgaz*). The vehemence of these references goes far beyond the degree of mere halakhic or philosophical value structures. They reflect the influence of the Toledano reforms of 1280–1281, in which the Castilian community, under the leadership of Todros Abulafia, imposed social restrictions designed to combat the excesses of Jewish slave owners with their gentile maidservants. This attribution of the archetypal qualities of the demonic to these four examples of forbidden intercourse indicates the kabbalistic support for these ethical reforms. (See Baer, *A History of the Jews in Christian Spain,* vol. 1 pp. 243–305, and "Ha-Reqa' ha-Histori shel ha-*Ra'aya Meheimna,*" pp. 1–44; Goldreich, "La'az Iberi be-Fragment Bilti-Yadu'a shel Ba'al *Tiqqunei ha-Zohar,*" p. 108.)

The author of the *Tiqqunim* continues the Zohar's characteristic ambivalence toward the feminine (TZ 133a). He respects the economic advantages of married life (TZ 30b, 126b), yet the wife is little more than the body to the husband's "soul" (TZ 134a). An unhappy marriage can lead to the total disruption of one's life (TZ 30b, 72a), yet a man is flawed without a wife, abandoned by God (TZḤ 114d). Communication with ones spouse wards off the demonic aspects of feminine sexuality (RM III 276a, see Z II 28). In the manner of the *Bahir,* marital ruptures, such as divorce or levirate marriage, are seen as metaphors for the chaotic upheavals in the cosmos (TZ 61a-b, 72a; see also Liebes, "Ha-Masiaḥ shel ha-Zohar," p. 203n.). The three guarantees of the marriage contract reflect triunity (TZ 22a–b), while the seven blessings of the wedding service reflect the seven lower *sefirot* (TZ 84a, see *Ketubot,* 7b–8a).

The author echoes the great biblical literary equation of idolatry with promiscuity (RM III 90a, 110a) as well as the Talmud's equation of idolatry with witchcraft. Illicit sexuality is idolatry, hence intercourse during the menstrual cycle is like a sacrifice to idols. These demonic qualities are a classical example of the negative elementary character of the Mother archetype (TZ 69a; see Neumann, *The Great Mother,* pp. 147–179).

103. I (TZ) 27a.
104. A reference to the demiurge Metatron.
105. Cf. Rashi to Genesis 2:18.
106. I (TZ) 27b.
107. RM III 216a, 276b; TZ 14b; TZḤ 98a.
108. TZ 14b.

109. I (TZ) 27a.
110. TZ 45b, 48a; TZḤ 99c.
111. TZḤ 99c. See TZ 5b, 45b; RM III 29b.
112. TZ 14b, 43b; RM III 254a; TZḤ 107b.
113. RM III 215a-b. See also TZ 53b.
114. TZ 48b.
115. *Berakhot,* 11a.
116. TZḤ 111d.
117. TZ 75a, 14b; TZḤ 111c–d; RM III 238b.
118. TZ 99a.
119. TZ 75a.
120. TZ 46a, after *Avot,* 5:7.
121. TZ 70a.
122. RM 275b–278a. See also Tishby, MhZ II, p. 385.
123. See also TZ 1b, RM III 64, 254a.
124. See also TZḤ 98a.
125. TZ 46b, see Tishby, MhZ II, p. 386.

Chapter Six Notes

1. "The Meaning of the Torah in Jewish Mysticism," in *On the Kabbalah and Its Symbolism,* p. 32. See also Frank Talmage, "Apples of Gold;" in Arthur Green, ed., *Jewish Spirituality,* vol. 1, pp. 333–344.
2. TZ 146a; RM III 278b, 279a, 281a.
3. *Berakhot,* 28a; Z II 272b; TZ 5a.
4. RM III 28b.
5. RM III 82b.
6. RM II 114a–b.
7. RM III 179a, 253a.
8. RM III 83a,
9. RM II 43a; III 245a–b, 273a. See *Pirqei de-Rabbi Eliezer,* 19.
10. *Berakhot,* 51a; TZ 61a, 84b.
11. TZ 132a.
12. TZ 41a.
13. There is a notion of ten *sefirot* contained in every *sefirah* (TZ 84a, 116b, 125b, 135a). This multiplicity of sefirotic possibilities enabled subsequent exegetes of the Zohar, particularly Moshe Cordovero, to resolve the textual contradictions that resulted from the various stages of the development of Zoharic theosophy. It also provided a way of imposing Lurianic understandings onto Zoharic texts. Other meditations on the number ten include TZ 31a (on tithes). See also TZḤ 109b.

14. RM II 115b–116a. In 115b, n. 14, Reuven Margoliot discusses the instances of this phenomenon across theosophical Kabbalah.

15. RM II 117a.

16. RM III 27b, 110a.

17. RM II 117a.

18. TZ 131b, 147a–b.

19. RM III 275b.

20. "The demonic is empowered by human sin." Daniel C. Matt, "The Mystic and the Miẓwot," in Green, ed., *Jewish Spirituality,* vol. 1, p. 388.

21. RM III 125b.

22. RM III 280a.

23. I (TZ) 27b.

24. Meaning that they have the same *gematria* (numerical coefficient: 207) as.

25. RM III 28b. See also *Sotah,* 21a, TZ 52b, TZḤ 97a.

26. Cf. Scholem, *Jewish Gnosticism, Merkabah Mysticism and Talmudic Tradition,* p. 11.

27. See Maimonides's *Guide for the Perplexed,* 3:47.

28. TZ 140a.

29. The broken notes blown with the *shofar.*

30. TZ 139b.

31. See Tishby, MhZ II, pp. 206–210; Z II 184b–185a; III 102a, 197a; RM III 237b.

32. TZ 62b.

33. TZ 23b; RM III 111a.

34. TZ 97b.

35. Z II 257b.

36. *Qol demamah daqah,* a three-part phrase.

37. I Kings 19:12. See TZḤ 107c.

38. RM III 279a. See also Talmage, "Apples of Gold;" pp. 330–331, which presents several examples of associative groupings of four fold entities.

39. Cf. *Baba Batra* 175b: "He who wishes to become wise, let him preoccupy himself with civil law (*dinei mammonot*)."

40. RM III 118a, also Liebes, *Peraqim be-Millon Sefer ha-Zohar,* p. 47; Tishby, MhZ I, pp. 346–348; *Or Yaqar,* vol. 15, pp. 164–167.

41. Literally, *DINA de-malkhuta DINA;* i.e., the law of the government is law. Here this is transformed to mean "the law of the *sefirah malkhut* is law."

42. RM II 118a.

43. Ibid.
44. Ibid.
45. This is also found in Z I 29a.
46. RM II 118a.
47. See *Baba Kamma,* 83b.
48. Apparently through faith healing.
49. RM II 118b
50. Ibid.
51. Ibid.
52. *Baba Kamma,* 26a
53. RM II 118a.
54. RM II 118a; TZ 59b.
55. TZḤ 110b; RM III 27b.
56. See Matt, *Zohar—The Book of Enlightenment,* pp. 38–39.
57. TZ 114a; TZḤ 121b; RM III 275b.
58. See also RM III 272a. This image is invoked by the *yenuka,* the wonder child, in Z III 189. See also Alexander Altmann, *Essays in Jewish Intellectual History,* pp. 161–179; Tishby, MhZ I, pp. 298–301.
59. This is a play on the Hebrew *yad* (read here as *yud*) *al kes yah* (the phonetic rendering of the letter *hey,* reversed).
60. RM II 120b, see also TZḤ 113c. According to Cordovero, the five species of grain are linked to the typologies of the scholar: saint, hero, Master of the Torah, seer, and prophet (see *Or Yaqar* 15, pp. 173–175; *Or ha-Ḥamah* II, 152a).
61. TZ 114a. See also Elliot Wolfson, "Dimmui Antropomorphi ve-Simboliqah shel ha-Otiyyot be-Sefer ha-Zohar" [Anthropomorphic Imagery and Letter Symbolism in the Zohar], in Joseph Dan, ed., *The Zohar and Its Generation,* p. 155n.
62. See *Targum Job,* 28:3, *Hagigah,* 12a.
63. RM III 227a.
64. TZ 31a, see *Berakhot* 40a.
65. RM II 120b, III 272a.
66. Elliot Wolfson has demonstrated that the author's understanding of the apotropaic function of circumcision originates with the German pietists. See his "Circumcision and the Divine Name," 108–110; and "Circumcision, Vision of God and Textual Interpretation, From Midrashic Trope to Mystical Symbol," *History of Religions* 27 (1987–1988): 198–215. See also Liebes, *Peraqim be-Millon Sefer ha-Zohar,* p. 274.
67. TZ 66b.
68. TZ 116b, 119b. See Z II 111b. See also *Shoḥer Tov,* 9:7; *Avot de-Rabbi, Natan,* 2:5.

69. *Romi Ravta and Romi Zeirta;* TZ 78a; TZḤ 120a.

70. TZ 78a. See also TZ 11a, 70a; *Bereshit Rabbah,* 21:9. On the homoerotic aspect of *meẓiẓah,* see Sander Gilman, *The Jew's Body* (New York: Routledge, 1991), p. 93.

71. TZ 11a, 69b, 78a; *Hagigah,* 11b–12a.

72. TZḤ 117b. See also TZ 11a, 78b; RM III 44a.

73. RM III 43b. See *Pirqei de-Rabbi Eliezer,* 29.

74. TZḤ 117b, see in particular *Tanḥuma,Va-Yera,* 6: "*Offspring shall serve him* (Psalms 22:31). R. Isaac said, Circumcision is called 'service' and sacrifices are called 'service.' The sacrificial service is with blood and the circumcision is with blood. Why does it say *Offspring will serve him?* When a man gives a drop of blood in circumcision it is beloved by the Holy Blessed One like a sacrifice."

75. TZ 11a; see *Shemot Rabbah,* 5:8.

76. TZ 121a–b; Z III 127b; see Judah Ḥayyat's commentary, *Minḥat Yehudah,* to *Ma'arekhet ha-Elohut,* p. 34. See also Moshe Idel, *Kabbalah: New Perspectives,* pp. 112–122, 330n.

77. See Yehudah Liebes's impressive monographs, "Ha-Mashiaḥ shel ha-Zohar," "Ha-Mitos ha-Kabbali she-be-fi Orpheos," and particularly "Keiẓad Nitḥabber Sefer ha-Zohar?" [How Was the Zohar Composed?], in Dan, ed., *The Zohar and Its Generation.* See also the entry *Idra* in Liebes's *Peraqim be-Millon Sefer ha-Zohar,* pp. 95–97. *Tiqqunei ha-Zohar* provides a gloss of the *Idrot* in TZ 121a–135b, see also RM III 275a. See also Tishby, MhZ I, p. 156; Scholem, *On the Kabbalah and Its Symbolism,* p. 104.

78. See Moshe de-Leon, *Sefer ha-Rimmon,* ed. Elliot Wolfson, (Atlanta: Scholars Press, 1988), pp. 3–9.

79. "Keiẓad Nitḥabber Sefer ha-Zohar?" pp. 13–46.

80. TZ 50b. See Moshe Idel, "Tefisat ha-Torah be-Sifrut ha-Heikhalot ve-Gilguleha ba-Kabbalah" [The Concept of the Torah in Heikhalot Literature and Its Metamorphoses in Kabbalah], *Jerusalem Studies in Jewish Thought* 1 (1989): pp. 59–60.

81. TZ 107b, 130a, 140b.

82. TZ 135b.

83. RM III 109b.

84. RM III 123b.

85. TZ 90b.

86. RM III 278b.

87. RM III 123b.

88. TZ 32a; TZḤ 101b. This is a classic kabbalistic principle described in the liturgical *PataḥEliyahu* (TZ 17a), in which the sefirotic tree is superimposed over the human form. See Arthur Green, *Tormented Master: A Life of Rabbi Nahman of Bratzlav,* p. 77.

89. TZḤ 101b; TZ 25b, 60a. See also TZ 50b, 52b, 107b, 116a; RM III 109b, 218b, 227b. See Liebes, *Peraqim be-Millon Sefer ha-Zohar,* pp. 86, 173, 203, 251–254; also Daniel Matt "The Mystic and the Miẓwot" p. 387.

90. TZ 131a.

91. Apparently, Metatron.

92. TZ 131a.

93. TZ 131a; RM III 82b.

94. RM III 16b; see *Kallah Rabati,* 3 ("All his sins are written on his bones, all his merits, on his right hand"). See Reuven Margoliot, *Niẓoẓei Zohar,* on TZ 81a, note 7, and Z II 151a, note 5, as well as *Sha'arei ha-Zohar,* p. 116a.

95. Cf. *Hagigah,* 12a.

96. TZ 139b.

97. RM III 257b; TZ 14b, 100b; TZḤ 117c. See also *Shemot Rabbah,* 52:3; *Va-Yiqra Rabbah,* 18:1, 27:1; *Qohelet Rabbah,* 12:5; Shabbat, 152a; *Baba Batra,* 83a; *Tanḥuma Emor,* 6.

98. See Matt, "The Mystic and the Miẓwot," pp. 383–384; Tishby, MhZ II, pp. 183–215.

99. RM II 158a, see *Tanḥuma Pequdei,* 3: "The Tabernacle is compared to the the whole world, and to the creation of Adam, who is a little world. When the Blessed Holy One created His world, He created it as one born of woman. As one begins from the navel and then stretches from side to side, so the Blessed Holy One began to create His world from side to side, first the rock of the sanctuary, and from it the world was hewn . . ."

100. TZ 13b.

101. RM III 109a–b, 246a–b. These four watches are portrayed extensively in various Zoharic articles on the spiritual dynamics of the evening; see Margoliot, *Sha'arei ha-Zohar,* p. 6.

102. Matt, "The Mystic and the Miẓwot," pp. 383–384; see Tishby, MhZ II, pp. 183–215

103. RM II 118a; III 17a

104. RM III 254b; see Tishby, MhZ II, p. 202n.

105. *Avot,* 4:11.

106. RM II 17a.

107. The tradition of the *ḥayyot* (beasts) as executors of God's wrath extends back to the Merkavah tradition; see David Halperin, *The Faces of the Chariot,* pp. 121–125.

108. Aramaic *le-qarva,* as in the Hebrew *qorban,* sacrifice. On sacrifice as an act of unification, see Tishby, MhZ II, pp. 194–201.

109. TZ 139b.

110. Literally, a sacrifice whose worth is dependent on the material income of the sacrificer.

111. TZ 10a, 35a, 36a.
112. TZ 55b; Z III 180b.
113. RM III 17a, 27a, 247b; TZ 101b.
114. RM II 157b–158a.
115. RM III 224b, 274b.
116. RM III 28a. See Tishby, MhZ II, pp. 206–210.
117. RM III 248a.
118. RM III 29a.
119. RM III 110a, 254b; TZ 62b.
120. RM II 119a.
121. TZ 70a. See Moshe Cordovero, *Sefer Gerushin* (Jerusalem, 1962) 86, p. 116.
122. RM II 119a, III 29a; TZ 59a, 12a.
123. "For as the fish cannot live without water, so the scholar cannot live without Torah" (RM III 42a). See also TZ 59a; RM III 278b.
124. Z I 64b–65a; III 224b.
125. See *Guide for the Perplexed,* III, 26, 32; see Matt, "The Mystic and the Miẓwot," p. 372; Tishby, MhZ II, pp. 195–214.
126. RM III 110a.
127. RM III 27b, 254b; see also Tishby, MhZ II, pp. 213–214.
128. "The Female Body and Religious Practice in the Later Middle Ages," in Michel Feher, ed., *Fragments for a History of the Human Body, Part 1* (New York: URZONE, 1989), p. 195. In that same collection, see Charles Mopsik, "The Body of Engenderment in the Hebrew Bible, the Rabbinic Tradition and the Kabbalah," pp. 56–73. Bynum's study of the role of food, *Holy Feast and Holy Fast* (Berkeley: University of California Press, 1987), examines Christian notions of empowerment and embodiment. There are paradigmatic differences, of course, between Christological understandings that involve the emulation of suffering and the kabbalistic understanding of overlapping models of individual-God-sacrifice.
129. TZ 13b, 62b.
130. Literally, *ruaḥ,* meaning wind.
131. RM III 235a.
132. TZ 52a–b; RM III 232b.
133. TZ 140a.
134. RM III 232b; cf. Alexander Altmann, *Studies in Religious Philosophy and Mysticism,* p. 167. See also Liebes, *Peraqim be-Millon Sefer ha-Zohar,* p. 266.
135. RM III 110a.
136. See Proverbs 30:15. The term *give,* literally, *hav,* is the rabbinic rendering of a dog's bark.

137. Literally, *marah,* also meaning bile.

138. TZ 140b.

139. See *Shabbat,* 74a.

140. Cf. Margoliot to Z I (TZ) 27b, note 3. See also Maimonides's *Commentary to the Mishnah, Avot,* 2:6.

141. RM III 234a–b. See also TZ 49a, 53a; *Sotah,* 45b.

142. RM III 28b.

143. I (TZ) 27b; TZ 29b.

144. See Ḥayyim Vital's note, in the standard editions of the Zohar, on this textual emendation.

145. RM III 28b.

146. RM III 28b, 282a.

147. RM III 28a; see also Z III 235b–236a.

148. RM III 28b; see also 228a.

149. TZ 59b. Reuven Margoliot's comment in *Niẓuẓei Zohar* may be read critically to imply that the author's numbering of eighteen *sirkhot* is derived from the Talmud's numbering of eighteen *terefot,* or mortal wounds, that render an animal unfit for consumption. See also *Be'er La-ḥai Ro'i* on TZ 70a.

150. See *Tur Yoreh Deah,* 39: 4–7.

151. TZ 29a. See also *Bahir,* 83, 101, 155, 175–178.

152. *Sukkah,* 34b, 35b. The version given here is a rough paraphrase of the rabbinic source.

153. *Sukkah,* 29b

154. Literally, "eternal life," with the numerical value of the Hebrew *hai* equaling eighteen.

155. TZ 29a.

156. This quotation differs significantly from *Sefer Yeẓirah* 1:13. See Moshe Cordovero, *Perush ha-RaMaK le-Sefer Yeẓirah,* (Jerusalem, 1989); pp. 82, 1978; also Tsvi Hirsch Shapira, *Tiqqunei ha-Zohar 'im Be'er La-ḥai Ro'i,* (Jerusalem, 1964).

157. *Sukkah,* 37b.

158. TZ 29a.

159. TZ 23a; III 255a–256b.

160. TZ 2b, 56b. See also *Tanḥuma, Emor* 19 ("Know that the *lulav* is like the human backbone, and the myrtle is like the eyes, and the willow is like the lips and the *etrog* is like the heart"). See *Sukkah,* 29b, 32b; *Va-Yiqra Rabbah,* 30:14 ("The *lulav* is like a man's spine, the myrtle is like his eye, the willow resembles the mouth, and the *etrog,* the heart . . . "); and *Bahir,* 83, 155. See also Amos Goldreich, "La'az Iberi be-Fragment Bilti-Yadu'a shel Ba'al *Tiqqunei ha-Zohar,*" p. 103.

161. TZ 89b, 125b, 134a; RM II 118b.

162. *Berakhot,* 28b.

163. *Va-Yiqra Rabbah,* 30:14.
164. *Berakhot,* 30b.
165. *Berakhot,* 33a.
166. *Yoma,* 85b.
167. *Berakhot,* 12a.
168. TZ 37a; see also 33a, 123a, TZḤ 19a, 115a, 116d.
169. TZ 56b; *Sukkah,* 32a.
170. See *Sukkah,* 39b; *Rosh Ha-Shanah,* 14b.
171. *Sukkah,* 34b.
172. TZ 2b, 23a.

Chapter Seven Notes

1. RM III 243b, 279b; TZ 85a; ZḤ (TZ) 32a, 34a.

2. See Robert Goldenberg, "Law and Spirit in Talmudic Religion," in Green, ed., *Jewish Spiritality,* vol. 1, pp. 245–246. A thorough study of some Kabbalistic Sabbath motifs is Elliot K. Ginsburg's recent *The Sabbath in the Classical Kabbalah* (Albany: State University of New York Press 1989).

3. TZḤ 101d.

4. RM III 243b.

5. The word *tal,* "dew," has a numerical coefficient of thirty-nine, the number of actions forbidden on the Sabbath, as well as the prescribed number of lashes for corporal punishment. *Tal* commonly symbolizes the outpouring of Divine effluence in the Zohar.

6. Literally, "fathers of labor," implying central acts of labor.

7. RM III 243b.

8. Ibid.

9. TZ 57b, 69a, 85a; RM III 243b. TZ 143b discusses the ritual attending the Sabbath's departure. The material is presented in Ginsburg, *The Sabbath in the Classical Kabbalah,* pp. 259–262.

10. TZ 56b–57a.

11. TZ 57a.

12. *Shabbat,* 118b.

13. TZ 57a–b.

14. TZ 57b. See also TZ 101a, 103a; TZḤ 113d.

15. *Pesaḥim,* 50a.

16. That is to say, indirectly (Hebrew: *ke-le-aḥar yad,* "with the back of the hand").

17. TZ 101a.

18. TZ 103a; see also TZḤ 114b.

19. RM III 244b–246b.

20. TZ 84a. See also Amos Goldreich, "La'az Iberi be-fragment bilti-yadu'a shel Baal *Tiqqunei ha-Zohar,*" p. 100.

21. *Berakhot,* 51a.

22. TZ 84b.

23. TZ 59a.

24. *Berakhot,* 46a.

25. TZ 84b; TZḤ 101a; RM III 244b.

26. RM III 245a.

27. RM III 244b–245a, 272a; TZ 31b, 84b; see *Yerushalmi Berakhot,* 6:1; *Berakhot,* 39b; *Shabbat,* 117b.

28. My thanks to Elliot Wolfson for this understanding.

29. RM III 244b.

30. RM III 244a.

31. RM III 216b; see *Bereshit Rabbah,* 98:9.

32. RM III 245b.

33. In each case, seventy.

34. RM III 216b.

35. TZ 72b; RM III 216b. See also *Avodah Zarah,* 33b.

36. RM III 245b, *Berakhot,* 28a. See earlier, pp. 00–00.

37. Elliot K. Ginsburg has identified the mythic validation of the Sabbath boundaries in three kabbalists: Joseph of Hamadan, Meir Ibn Gabbai, and the author of the *Tiqqunim.* (See *The Sabbath in the Classical Kabbalah,* pp. 222–224, nn. 244–245; and *Sod ha-Shabbat: The Mystery of the Sabbath* [Albany: State University of New York Press, 1989] pp. 21–22 and nn. 100–101.)

38. TZ 55b, 66b, 69a, 85b; TZḤ 107a; RM III 244a. The main sections of the Zohar, by comparison, do not examine the public and private domains, but rather the *teḥum Shabbat,* the boundaries within which one may walk on the Sabbath (see Ginsburg, *The Sabbath in the Classical Kabbalah,* pp. 221, 244n).

39. Literally, "There are four 'takings out' on the Sabbath" (*Shabbat,* 2a).

40. TZ 60a.

41. TZ 85a.

42. TZ 1b.

43. A metaphor for sexual chastity.

44. TZ 69a. See the explanation of Tsvi Hirsch Shapira, *Be'er La-ḥai Ro'i,* on the punishment of stoning, in which the stone sym-

bolizes the initial *yud* of the Divine name, representing the two highest *sefirot*.

45. TZ 57a.
46. TZ 77b.
47. TZ 69a, 92b.
48. TZ 60a, 69a, 85a; RM III 109a.
49. TZ 97b.
50. TZ 83b, 97b.
51. TZ 8a, 69a; Ginsburg, *The Sabbath in the Classical Kabbalah*, p. 224; and *Sod ha-Shabbat: The Mystery of the Sabbath*, p. 21
52. *Eruvin*, 2a.
53. TZ 8a.
54. RM III 122a.
55. I (TZ) 24a.
56. RM III 121b, 224a; TZ 36a.
57. Literally "the beginning of . . . "; in this case, "the beginning of wisdom" (Proverbs 4:7).
58. Literally, *vav.*
59. TZḤ 115a.
60. *Berakhot*, 12a.
61. *Berakhot*, 30b; TZḤ 109a.
62. TZ 136b.
63. TZ 8a, 14a, 46b.
64. TZ 14a.
65. *Sukkah*, 37b.
66. RM III 229a.
67. TZ 35a.
68. TZ 8a; RM III 271a; TZḤ 109a.
69. TZḤ 115a.
70. *Baba Batra*, 25b; see also *Shulkhan 'Arukh Oraḥ Ḥayyim*, 94:2. In the *Tiqqunim*, see I (TZ) 26b, 253b; RM III 28a; TZ 3b, 5b, 13b, 15a, 25b, 35a, 64b, 77a, 105a, 107a, 121b, 126b; TZḤ (TZ) 32c, 33c; TZḤ 98d, 109a. See also Margoliot, *Sha'arei ha-Zohar*, p. 181.
71. TZḤ 109a.
72. See Margoliot, *Sha'arei ha-Zohar*, p. 128; Scholem, *Jewish Gnosticism*, p. 16n.
73. I (TZ) 253b.
74. I (TZ) 26b.
75. TZ 5b, 126b. See also Z II 175b.

Conclusion Notes

1. TZ 6a, 133b–134a. See also Z I 199a.

2. A classic example would be the Zohar's interpretation of blowing the *shofar* on the New Year (Z III 88b).

Bibliography

Zohar

Zohar and Tiqqunim

Buzaglo, Shalom. *Tiqqunei ha-Zohar 'im Perush Kisse Melekh.* Jerusalem, 1903.

Elijah of Vilna. *Tiqqunei ha-Zohar 'im Bi'ur ha-GR"A* . Vilna, 1877.

Margaliot, Reuven. *Sefer ha-Zohar,* 3 vols., 4th ed. Jerusalem: Mossad HaRav Kook, 1964.

———, ed. *Zohar Ḥadash.* Jerusalem: Mossad HaRav Kook, 1978.

———, ed. *Tiqqunei ha-Zohar.* Jerusalem: Mossad HaRav Kook, 1978.

Shapira, Tsvi Hirsch. *Tiqqunei ha-Zohar 'im Perush Be'er La-Ḥai Ro'i.* Jerusalem, 1964.

Tiqqunei ha-Zohar. Bzhitomir, 1873.

Tiqqunei ha-Zohar . Orta Koj, 1740.

Commentaries on the Zohar and Tiqqunim

Azulai, Abraham. *Sefer Or ha-Ḥamah.* Jerusalem, 1876.

———. *Sefer Or ha-Levanah.* Premishla, 1899.

Buzaglo, Shalom. *Sefer Miqdash Melekh.* Amsterdam, 1766.

Cordovero, Moses. *Sefer Or Yaqar.* Jerusalem, 1972.

Elijah of Vilna and His School. *Kovez̤ Perushim al Sefer ha-Zohar.* Jerusalem: Makor, 1972.

Emden, Jacob. *Zoharei Ya'avez̤*, ed. Abraham Bick. Jerusalem: Da'at Torah, 1976.

Frisch, Daniel. *Oz̤ar ha-Zohar.* Jerusalem, 1976.

Horovitz, Zvi Hirsch. *Aspaqlaria ha-Meirah* . Fiorde, 1732.
Lavi, Shimon. *Sefer Ketem Paz,* Djerba, 1937.
Margoliot, Reuven, *Nẓoẓei Zohar* in *Sefer ha-Zohar,* Reuven Margoliot, eb. (as above).

Relevant Kabbalah

Altshuler, Aaron Meyer. *Kelalei Hatḥalat ha-Ḥokhmah.* Warsaw, 1893.
Azriel of Gerona. *Perush ha-Aggadot le-Rabbenu Azriel,* ed. by Isaiah Tishby. Jerusalem, 1945.
Azulai, Abraham. *Ḥesed le-Avraham.* Lvov, 1873.
Cordovero, Moses. *Or Ne'erav.* Jerusalem: Research Center of Kabbalah, 1982.
———. *Perush ha-RaMak le-Sefer Yeẓirah* . Jerusalem, 1989.
———. *Sefer Elimah Rabbati.* Hebron:, 1879.
———. *Sefer Pardes Rimmonim.* Munkatch, 1872.
———. *Shi'ur Qomah.* Jerusalem, 1974.
———. *Tefillah le-Moshe* [A Prayer for Moses]. Premishla, 1892.
David ben Yehudah he-Ḥasid. *Sefer Mar'ot ha-Ẓove'ot* (The book of mirrors). Edited by Daniel Chanan Matt. Chico: Scholars Press, 1982.
De Leon, Moshe. "Maskiyyot Kesef," ed. by Jochanan Wijnhoven. Master's thesis, Brandeis University, 1961.
———. *Sefer ha-Rimmon,* ed. by Elliot Wolfson. Atlanta: Scholars Press, 1988.
———. *Sheqel ha-Qodesh,* ed. by A. W. Greenup. London, 1911.
———. *Shushan 'Edut,* ed. by Gershom Scholem. *Koveẓ 'al Yad* 8 (1975): 325–70.
———. *Sod 'Eser Sefirot Belimah,* ed. by Gershom Scholem. *Koveẓ 'al Yad* 8 (1975): 371–384.
Ergas, Joseph. *Sefer Shomer Emunim.* Amsterdam, 1736.
Gikatilla, Joseph. *Sefer Ginnat Egoz.* Jerusalem: Yeshivat ha-Ḥayyim ve-ha-Shalom, 1989.
———. *Sefer Sha'arei Orah.* Warsaw, 1883.
Horovitz, Shabbatai Sheftal. *Sefer Shefa' Tal.* Lemburg, n.d.
Ibn Gabbai, Meir. *'Avodat ha-Qodesh.* Jerusalem, n.d.
Joseph of Hamadan. "Sefer TaShaq," ed. Jeremy Zwelling. Doctoral thesis: Brandeis University, 1975.
Margaliot, Reuven, ed. *Sefer ha-Bahir.* Jerusalem: Mossad ha-Rav Kook, 1978.
Ma'arekhet ha-Elohut. Mantua, 1558.
Naḥmanides. *Kitvei ha-Ramban,* vols. 1 and 2, ed. Ḥaim Dov Chavel. Jerusalem: Mossad ha-Rav Kook, 1965.

———. *Perush ha-Torah le-Rabbeinu Moshe ben Naḥman,* vols. 1 and 2, ed. Ḥaim Dov Chavel. Jerusalem: Mossad ha-Rav Kook, 1959.

Sefer ha-Qanah Cracow. 1894.

Sefer ha-Peliah. Koreẓ, 1883.

Vital, Ḥayyim. *Peri Etz Ḥayyim* (Jerusalem: Kabbalah Research Center 1964)

Yalkut ha-Ro'im. Jerusalem: Levin Epstein, 1973.

Yellish, Jacob Zvi. *Qehillat Ya'aqov.* Lemburg, 1870.

Secondary Sources

Alter, Robert. "Jewish Mysticism in Dispute." *Commentary* (September 1989): 53–59.

Altmann, Alexander. *Essays in Jewish Intellectual History.*: Hanover, N.H. University Press of New England, 1981.

———. *Studies in Religious Philosophy and Mysticism.* Ithaca, N.Y.: Cornell University Press, 1969.

Bacher, Wilhelm. "Judaeo-Christian Polemics in the Zohar." *Jewish Quarterly Review* 3 (1891): 781–784.

Baer, Yiẓḥak. *A History of the Jews in Christian Spain,* 2 vols. trans. Louis Schoffman. Philadelphia: Jewish Publication Society, 1978.

———. "Ha-Reqa' ha-Histori shel ha-*Ra'aya Meheimna*" [The Historical Context of the *Ra'aya Meheimna*]. *Zion* 5 (1940): 1–144.

Ben Shlomo, Joseph. *Torat ha-Elohut shel R. Moshe Cordovero* [The Nature of the Divine According to R. Moshe Cordovero]. Jerusalem: Bialik, 1965.

Biale, David. *Gershom Scholem: Kabbalah and Counter-History.* Cambridge, 1979.

Blickstein, Shlomo. "Between Philosophy and Mysticism: A Study of the Philosophical-Qabbalistic Writings of Joseph Gikatilla". Doctoral thesis, 1983.

Chernus, Ira. *Mysticism in Rabbinic Judaism.* Berlin: Walter De Gruyter, 1982.

Cohn-Alloro, Dorit. *Sod ha-Malbush u-Mareh ha-Melekh be-Sefer ha-Zohar* [The Secret of the Garment and the King's Image in the Zohar]. Jerusalem: Hebrew University Press, 1987.

Cooperman, Bernard Dov, ed. *Jewish Thought in the Sixteenth Century.* Cambridge, Mass.: Harvard University Press, 1983.

Dan, Joseph. "Samael, Lilit and the Concept of Evil in Early Kabbalah." *AJS Review* 5 (1980): 17–41.

———. *Torat ha-Sod shel Ḥasidei Ashkenaz* [The Esoteric Traditions of the German Ḥasidim]. Jerusalem: Bialik, 1968.

———, ed. *The Zohar and Its Generation,* Jerusalem Studies in Jewish Thought 8. Jerusalem: Magnes Press, 1989.

———. and Frank Talmage. *Studies in Jewish Mysticism*. Cambridge: Association for Jewish Studies, 1982.

Farber, Asi. "Iqvotav Shel Sefer ha-Zohar be-Kitvei R. Yosef Gikatilla" [Traces of the Book Zohar in the Works of R. Joseph Gikatilla]. *Alei Sefer* 9 (1981): 40–53.

———. "Li-Ve'ayat Meqoroteha shel Torato he-Qabbalit ha-Muqdemet shel R. Moshe de Leon" [On the Problem of Moshe de Leon's Early Kabbalistic Tradition]. Jerusalem Studies in Jewish Thought 1. Jerusalem: Magnes, 1981, pp. 56–76.

Gavarin, Martel. "Be'ayat ha-Ra' be-Qabbalat R. Yiẓḥak Sagi Nahor ve-Talmidav" [The Problem of Evil in the Thought of R. Isaac the Blind]. *Da'at* 26 (1987): 29–50.

Ginsburg, Elliot K. *The Sabbath in the Classical Kabbalah*. Albany: State University of New York Press, 1989.

———, ed. *Sod ha-Shabbat: The Mystery of the Sabbath*. Albany: State University of New York Press, 1989.

Goldreich, Amos "La'az Iberi be-fragment bilti-yadúa shel Ba'al Ra'aya Meheimna" in *The Zohar and its generation,* J. Dan; ed.

Gottlieb, Efraim. *Meḥqarim be-Sifrut ha-Kabbalah* [Studies in Kabbalistic Literature], ed. by Joseph Hacker. Tel Aviv: Rosenberg, 1976.

Green, Arthur, ed. *Jewish Spirituality,* vols. 1 and 2. New York: Crossroad, 1986, 1987.

———. "The Song of Songs in Early Jewish Mysticism." *ORIM* 2, no. 2: 49–63.

———. *Tormented Master: A Life of Rabbi Naḥman of Bratzlav*. Tuscaloosa: University of Alabama Press, 1979.

———. "The Ẓaddiq as *Axis Mundi*." *Journal of the American Academy of Religion* 45, no. 3 (1977): 327–347.

Gries, Zeev. "A Decade of Books on the Kabbalah." *Jewish Book Annual* 47 (1989).

Halperin, David. *The Faces of the Chariot*. Tubingen: J. C. B. Mohr, 1988.

Idel, Moshe. *Kabbalah: New Perspectives*. New Haven, Conn.: Yale University Press, 1988.

———. *Language, Torah and Hermeneutics in Abraham Abulafia*. Albany: State University of New York Press, 1989.

———. *The Mystical Experience in Abraham Abulafia*. Albany: State University of New York Press, 1988.

———. *Studies in Ecstatic Kabbalah*. Albany: State University of New York Press, 1988.

———. "Tefisat ha-Torah be-Sifrut ha-Heikhalot ve-Gilguleha ba-Kabbalah" [The Concept of the Torah in Heikhalot Literature and Its Metamorphoses in Kabbalah]. *Jerusalem Studies in Jewish Thought* 1 (1989).

Janowitz, Naomi. *The Poetics of Ascent*. Albany: State University of New York Press, 1989.

Katz, Jacob. *Halakhah ve-Qabbalah*. Jerusalem: Magnes, 1986.

Lieberman, Saul. *Hellenism in Jewish Palestine*. New York: Jewish Theological Seminary, 1950.

Liebes, Yehudah. "Ha-Mashiaḥ shel ha-Zohar" [The Messiah of the Zohar]. *In Ha-Ra'ayon ha-Meshiḥi be-Yisrael*. Jerusalem: Magnes Press, 1982, pp. 87–236.

———. "Ha-Mitos ha-Kabbali she-be-fi Orfeos" [The Kabbalistic Mythos in the Teaching of Orpheus]. *Jerusalem Studies in Jewish Thought* 7, no. 1, 1988.

———."Hashpa'ot Noẓriot 'al Sefer ha-Zohar" [Christian influences on the Zohar]. *Jerusalem Studies in Jewish Thought* 2, no. 1 (1982–1983).

Liebes, Yehuda "Keizad Nitḥabber Sefer ha-Zohar" ("How was the Zohar Written?") in J. Dan; ed. *The Zohar and its generation, Jerusalem Studies in Jewish Thought 8,* Jerusalem; Magnes 1989.

———. *Peraqim be-Millon Sefer ha-Zohar* [Some chapters in a Zohar Lexicon] Ph.D. dissertation, Hebrew University, 1976; Jerusalem: Hebrew University Press, 1982.

———. "Yonah ben Amitai ke-Mashiaḥ ben Yosef" [Jonah, Son of Amitai and the Messiah Son of Joseph]. *Jerusalem Studies in Jewish Thought* 3, nos. 1–2, (1983–1984).

Luria, David. *Kadmut Sefer ha-Zohar* [The Antiquity of the Zohar]. New York: Nezaḥ, 1951.

Margaliot, Reuven. *Sha'arei ha-Zohar*. Jerusalem: Mossad ha-Rav Kook, 1978.

Matt, Daniel Chanan. *Zohar—The Book of Enlightenment*. Ramsey, N.J.: Paulist Press, 1983.

Oron, M. "Qabbalat Castilea-Hemshekh O Mahapeḥa?" [The Kabbalah in Castile—Continuation or Revolution?). *Jerusalem Studies in Jewish Thought* 6: 383–392.

Scholem, Gershom. "The Concept of Kavunah in the Early Kabbalah." In *Studies in Jewish Thought,* ed. by Alfred Jespe. Detroit: Wayne State University Press, 1981.

———. "Ha-'Im ḥibber R. Mosheh de Leon et Sefer ha-Zohar?" [Did Moshe de Leon Write the Zohar?]. *Madda'ei ha-Yahadut* 1 (1926): 16–21.

———. "Ha-Ẓitat ha-Rishon min ha-Midrash ha-Ne'elam." [The First quotation from the Zohar's Midrash HaNe'elam]. *Tarbiẓ* 3 (1932): 181–183.

———. "Hitpatḥut Torat ha-'Olamot" [The Development of the Tradition of the worlds]. *Tarbiẓ* 2: 415–442; 3: 33–66.

———. *Jewish Gnosticism, Merkabah Mysticism and Talmudic Tradition*. New York: Jewish Theological Seminary of America, 1960.

———. *Kabbalah*. New York: Meridian Books, 1978.

———. *Major Trends in Jewish Mysticism*. 3rd ed. New York: Schocken Books, 1961.

———. "Mafteaḥ le-Perushim al 'Eser Sefirot" [A Key to Commentaries on the Ten *Sefirot]. Qiryat Sefer* 10 (1933–1934): 498–515; (1934): 39–53.

———. "The Name of God and Linguistic Theory of the Kaballah." *Diogenes,* nos. 79–80 (1972): 59–80, 164–194.

———. *On the Kabbalah and Its Symbolism*. New York: Schocken Books, 1965.

———. *Origins of the Kabbalah*. Princeton, N.J.: Jewish Publication Society and Princeton University Press, 1987.

———. "Parashah Ḥadashah min ha-Midrash ha-Ne'elam she-ba-Zohar." [A New Folio from the Zohar's Midrash HaNe'elam]. In *Sefer ha-Yovel li-Kevhod Levi Ginẓberg,* pp. 425–446. New York, 1946.

———. *Pirqei Yesod be-Havanat ha-Qabbalah u-Semaleha* [Essential Chapters in the Understanding of the Kabbalah and Its Symbolism), trans. by Joseph Ben Shlomo. Jerusalem, 1976.

———. *Reshit ha-Qabbalah* [Early Kabbalah]. Jerusalem, 1948.

———. *Sabbatai Ṣevi: The Mystical Messiah*. Princeton, N.J.: Bollingen, 1973.

———. "She'elot be-Viqqoret ha-Zohar mi-tokh yedi'otav al Ereẓ Yisra'el" (Questions in Zohar Criticism Based on Its Knowledge of the Land of Israel). *Ẓiyyon Meassef* 1 (1926): 40–55.

———."Te'udah Ḥadashah le-Toldot Reshit ha-Qabbalah" [A New Version of the Development of Early Kabbalah]. *Sefer Bialik* (1933): 141–162.

Sed-Rajna, Gabrielle. "Manuscrit du Tiqquney ha-Zohar." *Revue Etudes Juives* (1975): 162–175.

Septimus, Bernard. "Taḥat Edom ve-lo Taḥat Yishmael—Gilgulo Shel Maamar" [Better Under Edom than Ismael—The Transformation of an Expression]. *Zion* 47 (1982): 103–111

Shaḥar, Shulamit. "Ha-Catarism ve-Reshit ha-Qabbalah be-Lanquedoc" [Catharism and the Beginnings of the Kabbalah in Lanquedoc]. *Tarbiẓ* 40 (1971): 483–507.

——— and Fischel Lachover. *Mishnat ha-Zohar* [The Teaching of the Zohar], 2 vols. Jerusalem: Mossad Bialik, 1971.

Tishby, Isaiah. *Ḥikrei Qabbalah u-Sheluḥuteha* [Studies in the Kabbalah and Its Branches). Jerusalem: Magnes Press, 1982.

———. *Netivei Emunah u-Minut* [Paths of Faith and Heresy]. Jerusalem: Magnes Press, 1982.

Twersky, Isadore, ed. *Rabbi Moses Naḥmanides (Ramban): Explorations in His Religious and Literary Virtuosity.* Cambridge, Mass.: Harvard University Press, 1983.

——— and Bernard Septimus, eds. *Jewish Thought in the Seventeenth Century.* Cambridge, Mass.: Harvard University Press, 1987.

Wolfson, Elliot. "Biblical Accentuation in a Kabbalistic Key: Mystical Interpretation of the Ta'amim." *Journal of Jewish Liturgy and Music* (1988–1990) 21: 1–15; 22: 1–13.

———. "By Way of Truth: Aspects of Naḥmanides' Kabbalistic Hermeneutic." *AJS Review* 14 (1989): 103–178.

———. "Circumcision and the Divine Name: A Study in the Transmission of an Esoteric Doctrine." *Jewish Quarterly Review* 78, nos. 1–2. (July–October 1987): 77–112.

———. "Circumcision, Vision of God and Textual Interpretation, From Midrashic Trope to Mystical Symbol." *History of Religions* 27 (1987–1988): 198–215.

———. "Female Imaging of the Torah: From Literary Metaphor to Religious Symbol." In *From Ancient Israel to Modern Judaism: Intellect in Quest of Understanding: Essays in Honor of Marvin Fox,* vol. 2. Atlanta: Scholars Press, 1990, pp. 271–307.

———. "Left Contained in Right: A Study in Zoharic Hermeneutics." *Association for Jewish Studies Journal* 11 (1987): 27–51.

———. "Light Through Darkness: The Ideal of Human Perfection in the Zohar." *Harvard Theological Review* 81 (1988): 78–84.

———. "The Hermeneutics of Visionary Experience: Revelation and Interpretation in the Zohar." *Religion* 18 (1988): 311–345.

II. Mysticism

James, William. *The Varieties of Religious Experience.* New York: Modern Library.

Jonas, Hans. *The Gnostic Religion.* Boston: Beacon Press, 1958.

Katz, Steven, ed. *Mysticism and Philosophical Analysis.* Oxford: Oxford University Press, 1978.

———. ed. *Mysticism and Religious Traditions.* Oxford: Oxford University Press, 1983.

Matt, Daniel. "Ayin: The Concept of Nothingness in Jewish Mysticism." In *The Problem of Pure Consciousness: Mysticism and Philosophy,* ed. by Robert K. C. Forman. Oxford: Oxford University Press, 1990.
Neumann, Erich. "Mystical Man." In *The Mystic Vision*. Princeton, N.J.: Bollingen Press, 1968.
Nishitani, Keiji. *Religion and Nothingness*. Berkeley: University of California Press, 1982.
Otto, Rudolph. *The Idea of the Holy*. Oxford: Oxford University Press, 1923.
———. *Mysticism: East and West*. New York, 1959.
Rudolph, Kurt. *Gnosis: The Nature and History of Gnosticism*. San Francisco: Harper and Row, 1987.
Smart, Ninian. *Reasons and Faiths: An Investigation of Religious Discourse, Christian and Non-Christian*. London: Routledge and Kegan Paul Press, 1958.
Stace, W. T. *Mysticism and Philosophy*. Philadelphia:, 1960.
Staal, Frits. *Exploring Mysticism*. Berkeley: University of California Press, 1975.
Streng, Frederick J. *Emptiness: A Study in Religious Meaning*. New York: Abingdon Press, 1967.
Suzuki, D. T. *Mysticism: Christian and Buddhist*. New York, 1957.
Underhill, Evelyn. *Mysticism*. New York, 1955.
Woods, Richard, ed. *Understanding Mysticism*. New York: Image Press, 1980.
Zaehner, R. C. *Concordant Discord*. Oxford: Clarendon Press, 1970.
———. *Mysticism: Sacred and Profane*. Oxford: Clarendon Press, 1957.

III. Hermeneutics and Symbolism

Alter, Robert. *The Pleasures of Reading in an Ideological Age*. New York: Simon and Schuster, 1989.
Bloom, Harold. *Kabbalah and Criticism*. New York: Seabury Press 1975.
Boman, Thorlief. *Hebrew Thought Compared with Greek*. Philadelphia: Westminster Press, 1960.
Bynum, Caroline Walker. *Holy Feast and Holy Fast*. Berkeley: University of California Press, 1987.
Bynum, David. *The Daemon in the Wood*. Cambridge, Mass.: Harvard University Press, 1978.

Campbell, Joseph. *The Mythic Image*. Princeton, N.J.: Bollingen Press, 1974.

Derrida, Jacques. *Margins of Philosophy*. Chicago: University of Chicago Press, 1982.

Faur, Jose. *Golden Doves with Silver Dots*. Bloomington: University of Indiana Press, 1985.

Feher, Michel, ed. *Fragments for a History of the Human Body*, Parts 1 & 2 . New York: URZONE, 1989.

Freud, Sigmund. *The Interpretation of Dreams*, trans. by A. A. Brill. New York: Random House, 1950.

———. *Introductory Lectures on Psychoanalysis*. CPW vols. 15 and 16. London: Hogarth Press, 1963.

Frey-Rohn, Liliane. *From Freud to Jung*. New York: C. B. Putnam, 1974.

Gadamer, Hans-Georg. *Truth and Method*. New York: Crossroad, 1975.

Gilman, Sander. *The Jew's Body*. New York: Routledge, 1991.

Halivni, David. *Midrash, Mishnah and Gemara*. Cambridge, Mass.: Harvard University Press, 1986.

Handelman, Susan A. *The Slayers of Moses—The Emergence of Rabbinic Interpretation in Modern Literary Theory*. Albany: State University of New York Press, 1982.

———. "Fragments of the Rock: Contemporary Literary Theory and the Study of Rabbinic Texts—A Response to David Stern." *Prooftexts* 5, no. 1 (1985): 75–95.

Hartman, Geoffrey H. and Budick, Sanford, eds. *Midrash and Literature*. New Haven, Conn.: Yale University Press, 1986.

Heinemann, I. *Darkhei ha-Aggadah* [Ways of Aggadah], 3rd ed. Jerusalem: Magnes Press, 1970.

Heinemann, J. *Aggadah and Its Development: Studies in the Continuity of a Tradition*. Jerusalem: Keter, 1974.

Jung, C. G. "The Transcendant Function." In *The Portable Jung*, ed. Joseph Campbell. New York: Penguin Books, 1971.

———. *Aion*. CW 9a. Princeton, N.J.: Bollingen Press, 1953.

———. *The Archetypes and the Collective Unconscious*. Princeton, N.J.: Bollingen Press, 1959.

———. *Dreams*. Princeton, N.J.: Bollingen Press, 1974.

———. *Mysterium Coniunctionis*, CW 14. Princeton, N.J.: Bollingen Press, 1963.

———. *The Symbolic Life*, CW 18. Princeton, N.J.: Bollingen Press, 1963.

———. *Symbols of Transformation.* CW 5. Princeton, N.J.: Bolingen Press, 1956.

Lacan, Jacques. *Speech and Language in Psychoanalysis.* trans. Anthony Wilden. Baltimore: Johns Hopkins University Press, 1968.

———. *Ecrits: A Selection*, trans. Alan Sheridan. New York: W. W. Norton, 1977.

Ladner, Gerhart B. "Medieval and Modern Understandings of Symbolism: A Comparison." *Speculum* 54 (1979): 223–257.

Mattoon, Mary Ann. *Understanding Dreams.* Dallas: Spring, 1983.

May, Rollo, ed. *Symbolism in Religion and Literature.* New York: George Braziller, 1960.

Neumann, Erich. *The Great Mother.* Princeton, N.J.: Bollingen Press, 1955.

———. *The Origin and History of Consciousness.* Princeton, N.J.: Bollingen Press, 1954.

Neusner, Jacob. *What Is Midrash?* Philadelphia: Fortress Press, 1987.

Ozick, Cynthia. "Judaism and Harold Bloom." *Commentary* 67 (1979): 43–51.

Palmer, Richard E. *Hermeneutics.* Evanston, Ill.: Northwestern University Press, 1969.

Ricoeur, Paul. *Time and Narrative*, vols. 1 and 2. Chicago: University of Chicago Press, 1984.

Schneidau, Herbert. *Sacred Discontent: The Bible and Western Tradition.* Berkeley: University of California Press, 1976.

Scholem, Gershom. "The Name of God and Linguistic Theory of the Kaballah." *Diogenes* 79–80 (1972): 59–80, 164–194.

Silberer, Herbert. *Problems of Mysticism and Its Symbolism.* New York: Weiser, 1970.

Stern, David. "Literary Criticism or Literary Homilies? Susan Handelman and the Contemporary Study of Midrash." *Prooftexts* 5, no. 1 (1985): 96–103.

———. "Moses-cide: Midrash and Contemporary Literary Criticism." *Prooftexts* 4, no. 2 (1984): 193–204.

Wolosky, Shira. "Derrida, Jabes, Levinas: Sign—Theory as Ethical Discourse." *Prooftexts* 2, no. 3 (1982): 283–302.

Zunz, Y. L. *Ha-Derashot be-Yisrael*, trans. and revised by H. Albeck. Jerusalem: Bialik, 1954.

Index